# Listen to the Emerging Markets of Southeast Asia

# Listen to the Emerging Markets of Southeast Asia

## Long-term Strategies for Effective Partnerships

CORRADO G. M. LETTA

JOHN WILEY & SONS

Chichester · New York · Brisbane · Toronto · Singapore

National 01243 779777
International (+44) 1243 779777



*Other Wiley Editorial Offices*

John Wiley & Sons, Inc., 605 Third Avenue,
New York, NY 10158-0012, USA

Jacaranda Wiley Ltd, 33 Park Road, Milton,
Queensland 4064, Australia

John Wiley & Sons (Canada) Ltd, 22 Worcester Road,
Rexdale, Ontario M9W 1L1, Canada

John Wiley & Sons (Asia) Pte Ltd, 2 Clementi Loop #02-01,
Jin Xing Distripark, Singapore 0512

***Library of Congress Cataloging-in-Publication Data***
Letta, Corrrado G. M.
Listen to the emerging markets of Southeast Asia : long term strategies for effective partnerships / Corrado G. M. Letta.
p. cm.
Includes bibliographical references and index.
ISBN 0-471-96448-4 (cloth)
1. Europe—Foreign economic relations—Asia, Southeastern.
2. Asia, Southeastern—Foreign economic relations—Europe.
3. Investments, European—Asia, Southeastern. I. Title.
HF1532. 15.A785L48 1996
337.4059—dc20 96–22604
CIP

***British Library Cataloguing in Publication Data***

A catalogue record for this book is available from the British Library

ISBN 0-471-96448-4

Typeset in 11/13pt Palatino by Dobbie Typesetting Ltd, Tavistock, Devon.
Printed and bound in Great Britain by Bookcraft (Bath) Ltd, Midsomer Norton, Somerset.
This book is printed on acid-free paper responsibly manufactured from sustainable forestation, for which at least two trees are planted for each one used for paper production.

# Reviews

"The key sentence, describing at the same time the difficulties and the enormous opportunities in relations with Southeast Asia describes, the fascinating reality of a transcultural world: 'At least twelve different cultures in the EU member states—engaged in shaping a European culture—hope to co-operate with hundreds of cultures in Asia.' The study shows a Europe in search of new frontiers, in the traditions of Marco Polo, Vasco da Gama, and, since he was also looking for a seaway to Asia, Christopher Columbus. We are of course aware of the interest industrialists need to have in Asia: until the end of the decade, about 45% of world wide market growth (calculated in purchasing power parity) is expected to be generated in developing Asia. To participate with exports and investment in this growth matters for technical progress, for the economies of scale, and ultimately, for wealth and jobs in Europe. However, as the study indicates, Europe is late; hopefully this publication will help to speed up things. The author gives other good reasons for partnership: among other things he tries to explain why Europe matters for Asia."

**H. Oberhänsli,**
**Assistant to the Chairman for Economic Affairs, Nestlé SA**

"This study will contribute to a re-think amongst European decision makers on how to manage a win–win strategic business relationship with Southeast Asian nations in the next millennium."

**Ambassador Tony K. Siddique,**
**Economic Development Board, Singapore**

". . . eloquently portrays the Southeast Asian needs of today to build a better tomorrow and masterfully communicates them to European industrialists. We hope they listen, change their attitude and thus dramatically improve their ability and willingness to transfer their successes into our part of the world, accordingly."

**Mansor Abdullah, Director,**
**Malaysian Industrial Development Authority**

"The author gives a fundamental push to the European understanding of Asian countries. The right understanding at the right moment creates confidence—and confidence between Europe and Asia has to be built up so that they can manage together the future challenges to the advantage of both parties."

**Conrad B. R. Herrmann, Director,**
**Strategic Corporate Planning,**
**Phillipp Holzmann AG**

"Dr Letta has successfully combined extensive research about European companies 'doing business in Southeast Asia' with an in-depth knowledge of socio-cultural differences between the two regions, resulting in a book which should become a compulsory reference source for every European businessman pursuing success in Southeast Asia."

**J. E. Habibie,**
**The Ambassador of the Republic of Indonesia**

"Europeans have been reluctant to recognize, and then slow to react to the tremendous advances in the past 25 years of education, technical training and development potential in Southeast Asia. Given the labour-cost advantage that will work for many Asian countries for the foreseeable future, Europeans must develop a positive strategy for building on their remaining advantages by means of investment as well as licensing and co-operation agreements. A defensive strategy for retaining existing geographical or product markets is also necessary, but is also no longer sufficient."

**The Earl of Limerick KBE, Chairman,**
**Pirelli UK plc**

"For firms and businesses operating in 'fortress Europe', there is always a great deal to be learnt about competition and performance in the rest of the world. The volume constitutes a substantial contribution to deepening the knowledge and understanding of a vast and complex environment such as Southeast Asia. Those seeking new opportunities and open to the challenge of penetrating new markets will welcome the book; it has, among others, the unusual merit of combining the rigorous and analytical approach of research with plain and indeed communicative language."

**Luigi Marini,**
**UK Representative, Bank of Italy and Ufficio Italiano Cambi**

"Your point that Western Europe and the West European enterprises respectively will have to 'sell' themselves in Southeast Asia better than up to now, is certainly correct. I also know of cases where competing West European firms have failed in countries of Southeast Asia, not because their offers were inferior compared with those of their competitors, but because they were unable to establish a level of communication with their negotiating partners and therefore could not 'sell' themselves. You are certainly also correct in defining lack of knowledge of the other cultures concerned, and the attitude and approach resulting therefrom, as a causative deficit. I am certain that the present work will prove a valuable adviser for all those who wish to exploit their opportunities in the markets of Southeast Asia."

**Dr Rainer B. Gepperth, Director,**
**Deputy General Manager, Hanns Seidel Foundation,**
**Institute für Internationale Begegnung und Zusammenarbeit**

"The subject of your pragmatic investigation is very much part and parcel of the issues/problems Europe has to face and solve in building in the next millennium.

The depth and breadth of your research is simply amazing. It is, of course, the accurate input to the logical sequence of the development of your discourse. I am very glad that our conversations have been helpful to you.

The proposals you made to improve the competitiveness of the European construction industry in the International marketplace are very pragmatic and refreshing, and make a lot of sense.

The way you communicate—through the fluidity of your writing—makes this book very appealing from a cross-cultural communication point of view and an important tool for appealing and holding on to the minds of decision makers working in both the private and the public sectors in Europe and of practitioners of the international business scene."

**D. Verdiani, Director,**
**DGIII Industry, European Commission**

"There is a definite need for a better appreciation of Asian standards and values and this research should prove a valuable building block for management on both sides of the globe. I am certain that your book could serve as a catalyst for solid business relations between the two regions."

**Jesus P. Tambunting, Ambassador,**
**Embassy of the Philippines**

"I must admit, I found reading your publication very interesting and indeed most inspiring. It offers in fact, in a clear and straightforward way, a wide, comprehensive—and yet detailed—view of a very important and thought-provoking issue: the economic and cultural interaction between Europe and the countries of Southeast Asia, depicting, yes, the problems but also, and especially, the immense potential hidden in such business ventures.

Undoubtedly your study has identified—and offered some insightful advice on—the major difficulties encountered by businessmen in overcoming the different backgrounds and cultural barriers that quite often make ventures fail in their objectives. Indeed this research will prove to be an invaluable asset to companies, corporations and businesses alike whose interest at heart is that of seriously investing/co-operating with their Southeast Asia counterparts. The multicultural context and the flexibility, the unity in diversity, the reconciliation of differences: they are all concepts far too precious to be ignored, and they seem certainly to be the leit-motif of your research and its farsighted perspective!

It proves—and this I firmly believe—that on 'differences' we can only learn to grow, create and successfully interact."

**M. Stagno d'Alcontres,**
**CEO BdS Bank, London**

"First and foremost, I must commend you on the extent of your research and the depth of your analysis. Your observations on EU–ASEAN relations, your comments on cross-cultural attitudes and communication and the information provided on EU and national financial support were of particular interest.

Whilst this book is primarily aimed at developing commercial interest between Europe and Southeast Asia, we will, nevertheless, be pleased to keep it as a very useful reference tool in our Division."

**Donald J. Kerlin, Director,**
**International Maritime Organization**

"The United States and Europe are in a sort of international competition for Asian graduates studying abroad. The United States is winning hands down. Research by Corrado Letta of the Luigi Bocconi University in Milan shows that nearly ten times as many Chinese and Japanese students go to study in the United States as in Europe. America also attracts about three times as many South Koreans and students from the six ASEAN countries (Brunei, Indonesia, Malaysia, the Philippines, Singapore and

Thailand). Fewer than 35 000 students from the Far East studied in the big European countries in the most recent year for which figures were available (1988–89, alas): nearly 150 000 went to America.

It is worth remembering, too, that trade follows the diplomas. The Asian graduates will be the future generation of decision-makers in government and business when they return home. Already, in 1993, these same Asian countries exported between 1.4 and 2.3 times as much to the United States as to the European Union, which is a slightly larger market. When they next think about where to invest, where will they think of first?"

**The Economist**
**2 April 1995, page 50**

"The big challenge of Asian markets is one of the most difficult problems many European companies are trying to solve. This is particularly true for a number of Italian small and medium size enterprises which are dedicating a special effort to succeed in the area. This book can be a precious tool for designing the winning strategy for those companies, helping them to improve their competitive choices and to bridge the cultural and communication differences."

**Federico Galdi,**
**Director, International Affairs, Confindustria, Rome, Italy**

"Dr Letta's book is a very welcome source of information for forging increased economic cooperation between the two regions. I do believe successful partnership is based on understanding and trust among nations. Hence, I hope that this book will bring about greater European participation in Southeast Asia, resulting in mutual benefits."

**Dato Kassim Daud,**
**High Commissioner, Brunei Darussalam**

"The work by Dr Letta on the business relations between Southeast Asia and Europe is indeed interesting and inspiring. It provides in-depth studies on the economic and cultural interaction between the two regions, thereby furnishing European businessmen who are interested in penetrating the rapid growing Southeast Asian markets with up-to-date information."

**Anurak Thananan**
**Thailand Ambassador**

# Contents

# Foreword

The establishment of a truly multilateral trading system and the resulting liberalization of world trade feature prominently amongst the most meaningful events in international relations during the post-war period. These interrelated developments have deeply influenced the world in which we live, both with respect to people's material, as well as spiritual and political life. Over the years, ideas, cultures, technologies and economic progress have accompanied the exchange of goods and services. The development of transportation and telecommunications has accelerated further that new dimension between man and his lifestyle that today we call "globalization" of the world economy.

The data speaks for itself: from 1950 to date, international trade has grown by a yearly average rate of 6 per cent, while world output has grown by 4 per cent. The difference between these two figures constitutes the specific contribution of international trade to the interdependence of national economies and the globalization of the world economy.

It is within this framework of general growth of the world economy that we should look at the new realities of emerging countries and at the future prospects for developing countries. Perhaps, the most significant aspect to be considered here is the great change that has taken place in the direction of economic and trade policies in most developing countries in the period from early post-war to today. From protectionist policies that, in all these years, proved unable to resolve the problems of economic and social development experienced by many countries, we now see that, increasingly, these countries are moving towards open trade policies, based on "free market" principles and the respect of its rules.

This change of direction has been so significant in the last few years, that it is now a common view to consider that the most important outcome of the last round of multilateral trade negotiations, the Uruguay Round concluded in 1993, is to be found in the solid integration of most developing countries into the world trading system. More than three-quarters of the members of the World Trade Organization—currently 112 countries—are countries in development or economies in transition. A third of the top 25 exporting and importing nations are now developing countries. In the last 10 years, the trade share of industrial products from developing countries has doubled and today, exports of goods and services from these countries represent 25 per cent of world trade. Between 1980 and 1994, the 15 most dynamic countries, in terms of shares of world trade, were all developing countries. In the near future, around two-thirds of total world imports will be accounted for by developing countries.

There is no other area in the world where the effects of this economic integration have produced more spectacular results than in East Asia, the region analysed in Professor Letta's present book. In 1960, East Asia accounted for 4 per cent of world output, today it accounts for 25 per cent. The World Bank has calculated that, between 1992 and the year 2000, 40 per cent of all new purchasing power in the world will be created in this region. The regional economic outlook points to a further acceleration of economic growth of these countries and their increased role in the world economy.

However, it would be misleading to consider these countries only as major exporters and strong competitors in foreign markets. The truth is that these countries also represent the markets in which, in the coming years, the most rapid expansion of demand for goods and services will occur. In fact, this is already happening. Data in the last WTO Annual Report on international trade points out that, in the first six months of 1995, imports by East Asian nations have increased by 30 per cent, continuing to exceed the increase in their exports towards the rest of the world. Under these aspects, the inevitable conclusion is that the trading opportunities offered by these nations largely overcome any threat that is, in reality, the mere consequence of the continuing adjustment process that is required by the ever changing realities of world markets.

But there is another issue that deserves deep consideration: the regionalistic drive which is inherent in certain current conceptions of commercial relationships. In the specific East Asian case, it appears even more necessary, for a balanced development of the world trading system, that the extraordinary economic progress experienced by the Asian countries is not confined solely to this area, in terms of prevailing preferential treatments among only a few nations. The international community, and Europe particularly, has a major stake in ensuring that equitable prospects of growth are secure for all its members in the future. This can only be achieved by keeping any development of the trading relationships between Asian nations, as well as between Asian nations and other countries, compatible with parallel developments in the multilateral trading system. Only the multilateral trading system will be able, in the end, to sustain a world economic growth through the creation of a truly universal system, based on rules negotiated and approved by all countries and capable of allowing for predictable conditions of market access and investment.

In the foreground of this new reality of economic international life, Europe must accelerate the change of its approach towards the outside world, and especially towards Asia, by shifting from an "import-defensive" environment to an "export-orientated" strategy.

This book looks for answers to this major question.

Ambassador Renato Ruggiero
Director-General of the World Trade Organization

# Preface

To date, European businesses, unlike their counterparts in Japan and the United States, have made little unified attempt to establish an assertively strategic common presence in the emerging markets of Southeast Asia. This book poses the question of why the opportunities these markets present to the 15 member nations of the European Union have not been maximized—assessing properly and accepting the risks involved—despite an expressed willingness on the part of Asian businesses to be courted by European investors, and identifies strategic planning in the global economy and transcultural world; organization/financial engineering; human resources; flexibility; adaptability; co-ordination, political clout and cross-cultural communication as factors. The text considers the impact of these factors on the development of the vision, negotiations, and the process of sharing knowledge with the Asian partners. A mutually beneficial partnership can only be achieved through effective cultural communication, and the onus is on European businesses to take the initiative. They must learn to change their attitudes towards Asia from a short-term approach to a long-term one strategically planned with full respect for their potential Asian partners—venturing with them on an equal basis. This book examines some of the initiatives that might be taken to develop such a business relationship and proposes new business strategies for improving the performance of European transnational companies and medium-sized to small companies in the Southeast Asian region.

Why are Europe and Southeast Asia important to each other? The Association of South-East Asian Nations (ASEAN) and other Asian markets have expressed concern about the dominance of Japan ("Japan Inc.") and the United States ("USA Inc.") in the region and are looking to Europe to counterbalance their influence. For its part, European industry needs to adopt a similar approach by forging Europe Inc. if it is to compete on equal terms with its global competitors. The need of the emerging markets of Southeast Asia for European involvement in its businesses on a scale to match the involvement of Japan and the United States thus complements the need for Europe to redefine its role on the world stage in general. In this book, I have attempted to illustrate what could be done to satisfy both sets of needs.

Corrado G. M. Letta
SDA–Bocconi
Milan, Italy

# Acknowledgements

This book has profited from the advice, criticisms, suggestions, and remarks of many people.

First and foremost, my deepest gratitude goes to Ambassador R. Ruggiero, Director General, World Trade Organization (WTO), who in spite of his pressing and numerous world-wide commitments made time to write the foreword.

Dr D. Verdiani, Director, EU Commission DGIII-Industry, Brussels; Dr M. Stagno d'Alcontres, CEO, BdS Bank, London; and Mr Pierre Heilporn, Director General, Banque Bruxelles Lambert S.A., read the manuscript in its near-final form and made many perceptive suggestions for which I am indebted.

In addition to reading the fifth draft of the manuscript and making suggestions for improvements, Dr H. Oberhänsli, Assistant to the Chairman for Economic Affairs, Nestlé S.A., offered support by making available the research carried out by the European Round Table of Industrialists on strategies for achieving world-wide competitiveness in industry.

The comments of Dr Dieter Schreiber, Director General, Société Européenne de Construction S.A. in Brussels, particularly on the construction industry, were most helpful.

Professors V. Coda and M. Decastri, President and Director, respectively, of SDA–Bocconi and Professor C. Filippini, Director of the Instituto di Studi Economico Sociali per l'Asia Orientale (ISESAO) at Bocconi University in Milan, shared my vision and provided unconditional support and encouragement. I am indebted to Dr R. Ravagnani, also of that major European think tank that is SDA–Bocconi, for his helpful suggestions on how to present the vast amount of material concisely and logically.

The writing of this book was also supported, in one way or another, by the following people, to whom I express my thanks: Mr S. Sastrowardojo, Indonesian Minister for Foreign Investments; Professor Dr Wardiman Djojonegoro, Indonesian Minister of Education and Culture; Mr Richard N. Toub, American counsellor and attorney at law; Mr L. Marini, UK Representative, Bank of Italy and Ufficio Italiano Cambi; Lord Limerick, KBE, Chairman of Pirelli plc; Indonesian Ambassador to the UK, J. E. Habibie; the Philippines' Ambassador to the UK, J. P. Tambunting; Ambassador T. K. Siddique of the Singapore Economic Development Board; Mr M. Abdullah, Director, Malaysia Industrial Development Authority; Mr K. S. Leaf, Chairman, Burson–Marsteller International; Mr Ben L. Papé, Corporate Marketing, Pirelli Cables Ltd; Mr D. J. Kerlin, Director, International Maritime Organisation; Mr C. T. Kyzer, Business Development Manager, Far East, Bechtel Inc.; Dott. Federico Galdi, Director, International Relations Confindustria, Rome; P. Atkins, Manager, Hongkong Bank, Jakarta; Dr R. H. Wilcox, Center for Strategic & International Studies, Georgetown University, Washington D.C.; Mr J. R. Sharpe, Senior Vice President, Export–Import Bank of the United States, Washington D.C.; Mr C. F. Ray, Vice President, Atlantic Richfield Inc.; Mr M. Nor Jeludin, Chargé d'Affaires, Embassy of Brunei Darussalam to the EU; Dr Rainer B. Geppert, Director, Hanns Seidel Foundation, Munich; Professor Dr Walther Kebler, President der Fachhochschule, Munich; Mr Hans Heckart Scholz, Executive Director, Siemens AG, Munich; Dipl. Ing. Harisanto, President, P. T. Aparc, Bandung; Professor H. L. Tosi, Department of Management, University of Florida; Dr A. Corrias, Director General International Affairs, Istituto per la

Ricostruzione Industriale (I.R.I.), Rome; Dr L. Daina, Secretary General, Italy–Japan Business Group, Rome; Mr L. E. Kruse, Vice Consul, Royal Danish Consulate General, Milan; Dr E. Conte, Economic Attaché, Italian Embassy, London; Dr Alan Smith, Director, Academic Cooperation Association, Brussels; Mr Kamal Ismaun, Minister Counsellor, Malaysian Embassy, Brussels; Mr Rosli Ismail, First Secretary, Malaysian Embassy, Rome; Dr G. Kanter, Executive Director, Mr J. P. Vu, Manager Consulting Services, F. Phillips, Senior Country Officer, and Mr E. A. Wegeling, Economist, all of the Asian Development Bank, Manila; Ms N. Gourievidis, Head, ASEAN Department, Chambre de Commerce et d'Industrie de Paris; Dr P. E. Dewilde, Head, Education and Training Division, European Bank for Reconstruction and Development, London; and Mr G. Bagnasco, General Manager, Hotel Borobudur Intercontinental, Jakarta.

The wordprocessing assistance of Marie Florence Labrique during production of the second draft of the manuscript was a challenging and successful exercise in cross-cultural communication.

In particular I would like to thank Robyn Flemming without whose insight and editorial guidance this book would have been less focused.

Finally, I would like to express my gratitude to my editor, Diane Taylor, who understood my vision and ironed out many flaws in the flow of my arguments. Throughout the project, she and her interdisciplinary cross-cultural team challenged me at the right time, in the right way, and in the appropriate places.

# List of Acronyms

| | |
|---|---|
| ACA | Academic Cooperation Association |
| AFTA | Asia Free Trade Area |
| APEC | Asia Pacific Economic Cooperation |
| ASEAN | Association of South-East Asian Nations |
| Asem | Asia Europe Meeting |
| BC-Net | Business Cooperation Network |
| BIS | Bank for International Settlements |
| BRITE | European Research in Advance Material |
| CEO | Chief Executive Officer |
| EAGA | East Asia Growth Area |
| EATEC | Europe–Asia Environmental Technology Center |
| EBC | European Business Council |
| EBRD | European Bank for Reconstruction and Development |
| ECI | European Construction Industry |
| EFTA | European Free Trade Association |
| EIB | European Investment Bank |
| EIPP | European Investment Partners Programme |
| ERT | European Round Table (of Industrialists) |
| ESPRIT III | European Strategic Programme for Research in Technology |
| EU | European Union |
| EUREKA | European Research and Coordination Agency |
| FDI | Foreign Direct Investment |
| GATT | General Agreement on Tariffs and Trade |
| GDP | Gross Domestic Product |

| | |
|---|---|
| GNP | Gross National Product |
| GSP | Generalized System of Trade Preferences |
| HPAE | High Performance Asian Economies |
| IBRD | International Bank for Reconstruction and Development—known also as World Bank |
| ICI | Imperial Chemical Industries |
| IFC | International Finance Corporation |
| INDOSAT | Indonesian Satellite Communication |
| ISESAO | Istituto di Studi Economico Sociali per l'Asia Orientale |
| KBE | Knight Commander of the Order of the British Empire |
| MFN | Most Favoured Nation |
| NAFTA | North America Free Trade Agreement |
| NATO | North Atlantic Treaty Organization |
| NICs | Newly Industrialized Countries |
| OECD | Organization for Economic Co-operation and Development |
| R&D | Research and Development |
| SA | Strategic Alliance |
| SEC | Société Européenne de Construction |
| SMIT | Singapore–Malaysia–Indonesia Growth Triangle |
| SPRINT | Strategic Programme for Information and Technology Transfer |
| SRC | Self Reliance Criterion |
| TNC | Transnational Companies |
| UNMC | United Nations Center for Multinational Companies |
| WEF | World Economic Forum |
| WTO | World Trade Organization |

# Introduction

The aim of this book is to examine why European businesses have failed, to date, to claim a significant share of the Southeast Asian business contract pie and to propose long-term business strategies for forging a dynamic and assertive presence in both the Asian region and, by extension, in the global economy. On 1 June 1995, *Le Monde* published the article "Japon–Europe: Un Ignorance Reciproque" by Patrice de Beer, he stated also that

> "Le professeur Kenneth Courtis, stratège de la Deutsch Bank à Tokyo, se montre très sèvère sur le 'dèclin' de l'influence européenne en Asie: 'Le pouvoir économique est en trein de glisser vers l'Asie. L'Europe s'est up peu endormie, elle est trop lente à reagir aux changement dans le monde. Vue d'Asie elle parait petite, compliquée avec ses langues, ses cultures et ses traditions. Aucune multinationale européenne ne peut avoir de stratégie internationale sans prévoir 30% de son chiffre d'affaires en Extreme-Orient.'"*

Part I, "Mapping an Investment Strategy", contains three chapters. Chapter 1 discusses the nature of our global, transnational economy and transcultural world. We review the objectives of transnational companies and medium-sized to small companies in exploiting foreign markets, and the

---

*"Professor Kenneth Courtis—strategist at Deutsch Bank Tokyo—is very severe on the 'decline' of the European influence in Asia: 'The Economic power is sliding towards Asia. Europe seems to be sleepwalking, is too slow in reacting to changes in the world. From Asia it seems small, complex with its languages, its cultures and its traditions. No European multinational can have an international strategy without planning 30 per cent of its global turnover in the Far East.'"

opportunities that dictate the strategies and tools they adopt in order to achieve those objectives.

In Chapter 2 we examine the rationale for a co-operative framework between Europe and Southeast Asia. Most European businesses are unaware of the increasing importance in global terms of the emerging markets of the region, and thus are ignorant of the opportunities being presented to companies that are less backward in coming forward, notably American and Japanese companies. We identify some of the fears that Europeans and Asians have of each other, such as Europeans' fear of unfair competition from Asians, as well as other factors that inhibit European penetration of the region—in particular, the need for European companies to develop a collective vision for Asia, to put their organizational and financial engineering house in order. In attempting to define the likely future development of European Union–ASEAN co-operation, the chapter compares the two regions' processes of integration, trade, and financial flows, and discusses issues of security and leadership in Asia. It concludes that Europe must acknowledge the necessity for partnership with the Pacific community following the demise of communism in Europe and the consequent transformation of the Atlantic community.

In Chapter 3 we examine a number of different viewpoints on investing in Southeast Asia, and discuss how "risk" and "opportunity" may be considered a matter of perception. How we perceive a situation is determined by our culture, beliefs, and attitudes. An effective partnership between European and Southeast Asian business ventures is contingent upon the European partner altering its perception so that it more closely aligns with that of its Asian partner.

Part II of the book examines the management of cross-cultural communication. It focuses on the most critical factor in the success or failure of international joint ventures: the actual performance of the expatriate resident manager in the host country. Issues and problems include: understanding cultures, successfully negotiating and operating joint ventures in a cross-cultural context, and delegating decision-making authority.

Chapter 4 considers culture as an integral element of the communication process. We begin by considering that culture is all-encompassing, yet there is no one culture. We outline some of the major similarities and differences between Europe and Southeast Asia, and discuss the role of cultural and cross-cultural analysis as vital inputs to the development of a business relationship. Hence, possible areas of cross-cultural misinterpretation are identified. Much of the literature on culture and cross-cultural research has a Western focus: very little research has been done on cross-cultural situations in the individual emerging Asian markets.

Chapter 5 analyses the impact of cultural differences on negotiations and outlines what is required for European companies to clinch a joint venture deal in order to be able to operate in a particular country.

A number of conclusions can be drawn from the discussion in Part II, notably the necessity for European companies to make a critical switch in attitude from the short term to the long term, and from defensive protection of its markets from "unfair Asian competition" to aggressive co-operation on local cultural terms.

Part III, "Creating Europe Inc.", identifies new ways for European companies to learn how to effectively improve their performance in specific industries in Southeast Asia and thus on the global economic stage.

The main problems encountered by Europe Inc. in penetrating the Asian markets are identified in Chapter 6, and suggestions are made on how to turn past failures into future successes. Chapter 7, "Putting the House of Europe Inc. in Order", looks at the sweeping changes in attitude that are required in the areas of cross-cultural communication, organizational and financial engineering, service flexibility, strategic marketing, strategic alliances, and human resource management. The second part of the chapter outlines some practical initiatives for forging Europe Inc. and developing an organizational structure.

Chapter 8 highlights human capital as the main means of harvesting the highest long-term rewards. The chapter analyses the Asian "brain brigades", emphasizes the need for academic co-operation and management training programmes, and identifies the specific training needs of would-be European expatriate managers.

Chapter 9, the final part of the book, draws some global conclusions.

# Part I

## MAPPING AN INVESTMENT STRATEGY

# 1
# The Global Economy and Transculturalism

## INTRODUCTION

European companies willing to look to the emerging markets of Southeast Asia for their future growth must consider the global business environment in which they operate. They must take into account the respective roles of Asia — in particular, the emerging countries of Southeast Asia — and Europe in the global economy and the impact of transculturalism on those roles. Their need of each other as we move into the next millennium will be apparent to the astute among them, as will the fears that have moulded their business relations in the past. Further, they will need to be aware of the impact of political and managerial developments in both regions on their investment strategies.

The first part of this book focuses on the above factors, using a brushstroke approach to create a canvas on which both transnational and medium-sized to small companies in Europe can outline their strategies for penetrating the markets that are continuing to emerge in Asia.

## EVOLUTION OF THE GLOBAL ECONOMY

Stockbrokers' and currency dealers' long work days are dictated by the demands of the world's financial markets. The market doesn't wait for the broker who takes time off to attend his child's birthday party: it is ruthless and unrelenting. When the markets close in Tokyo (daily average trading US$126 billion in 1995[1]), Hong Kong (US$61 billion), and Singapore (US$76 billion), those in Europe (London US$300 billion; Switzerland US$36 billion) open, followed by New York (US$192 billion) and then back again to Tokyo.

The market is global, fast, and highly efficient. The Bank for International Settlements (BIS) estimated that US$880 billion was traded daily across national borders in computerized deals in 1995. The flow of capital is almost equivalent to the entire wealth produced in a year by a country such as France. The global market never closes, and its importance cannot be over-emphasized. To all intents and purposes, many consider it the police, judge, and jury of the world economy.

In addition to the financial markets, the transnational economy is characterized by its immunity from the influence of individual national governments—which can only respond to but cannot shape it, by the speed of transactions, the rapid spread of innovations, the global marketing of goods and services, and specialized education and training.

Thus we live in a transnational economy in which both transnational companies and medium-sized to small companies have a distinct role to play. According to the International Finance Corporation (IFC) transnational companies currently channel about 83 per cent of their investments towards rich countries. There has been little incentive to redirect investment towards developing countries and away from the rich markets where profits are greater and more readily achievable. The IFC, a World Bank affiliate, has analysed the rate of return in various regions, as follows: Europe, the Middle East, and North Africa 15.1 per cent; Asia 13.5 per cent; and Latin America and the Caribbean 11.1 per cent. Mr Will Berry, President of the European Chamber of

Commerce (ECC) commenting on the ECC's 1995 study on the status of the EU–US links stated: "more and more international companies are investing in new plants and equipment and creating jobs right here in the USA. Half of the jobs in the US created by the EU companies are in the high-wage manufacturing sector. Almost 3 million jobs in the US are directly supported by European investment with 2.5 million linked to exports to Europe."[2] The most common form of investment in developing countries is foreign direct investments in various forms of joint ventures (with or without equity participation), which allocate (or withhold) most of the resources needed for industrialization, especially technology. The problem has been that transnational companies prefer to put their own corporate interests first and to operate in a global context that offers returns in the short term, while the developing countries are more firmly based in a national context and offer potential returns in the longer term.

The evolution of the world's economies into a global economy over the last 40 years has had an impact comparable to that of tectonics in the field of geology. This comparatively recent and revolutionary view distinguishes six evolutionary stages of the earth's geological features from a single mass, called Pangae, into today's five continents. If this trend is projected into the future, earth scientists have suggested that East Africa will split along the line of the great river valleys, Australia will continue to drift northwards, and the Atlantic will open up further. The continued spreading of South America towards the Pacific Basin will cause it to override the southern East Pacific in much the same way that California has overridden its northern end.

In the same way, economic policy-making is increasingly shifting from the national state to the region via the creation of several levels of regional integration, including free trade areas, customs unions, common markets, and economic unions. These alliances are continuing to take shape, and to reshape the map of the world economy, because their fundamental aim is to improve the economic situation of the member states by reducing or eliminating nationalist obstacles to trade and investment. Free trade means solidarity with the developing countries which urges us to attack the exploitation of the poorest; protectionism is the equivalent of egoism, it means not to be willing to participate in the actual building up of a better world. Without profit there is no economic growth. The problem is not the profit but the distribution. For many years the liberalization of trade appeared to be the weapon western capitalism was using against the developing world. Instead today it is a request from the non-industrialized world in general and in particular Southeast Asian countries. This very loud request is made because they know that the only way to attract private capital—which creates new jobs—is to be able to export one's own products. Thus, this multilateral process stimulated a world-wide debate which lasted eight years. Called the GATT Uruguay Round after its inception in Punta del Est, Montevideo, Uruguay, in September 1986, the debate produced a 26 000-page document weighing 400 pounds which was ratified by 120 countries on 16 April 1994 in Marrakesh, Morocco, in front of 3000 delegates.

On 1 January 1995, the new organization spawned by the successful completion of GATT, the World Trade Organization (WTO) came into being. To ensure the growth of the world economy and world peace the opportunities the WTO aims to maximize—in the full understanding of the risks bind to them—are: the implementation of the GATT agreement; integrate developing countries in the global economy; resolve conflicts between economic interdependence and protectionism; to create adequate mechanisms to ensure that Regional Trade Groups comply with multilateral rules; to analyse the relationship between trade and the environment; to create consensus agreements on negotiations for the investment rules and the relationship between competition policy and trade. How do we achieve these goals?

On 1 May 1995, Ambassador Renato Ruggiero began his four year mandate as Director-General of the WTO. On the one hand he is powerless in achieving the goals of the global organization he leads. On the other hand, he is uniquely placed to achieve these goals using the only two powerful weapons at his disposal: security and persuasion.

By security it has to be understood that the WTO representing objectively the interests of all its 150 members has to create that climate of mutual trust in which its members feeling mutually protected and respect the multilateral system rules. Thus, it allows the WTO to continue in promoting more liberalization of trade and fight protectionism.

To persuade implies to educate the WTO's members to put aside their ways of seeing, perceiving, saying, doing and organizing themselves prior to their membership to the WTO and to learn a new understanding that will change their attitudes. Because security and world peace depend on the opening up of markets and policies towards developing countries, using the persuasion weapon, the WTO's Director-General aims at achieving two objectives. On the one hand, to increase the developing countries' understanding that all of us have the responsibility to be more rational and less emotional in terms of human rights and the protection of the environment. On the other hand, he aims at making industrialized countries accept the fact that a rapid integration of the developing countries into the global economy is of the utmost importance (precisely for reasons of growth of the global economy and world peace) and that these countries can afford to import more only if they are allowed to export more. Therefore, the OECD countries have to adapt themselves to this new reality by speedily restructuring their ways of seeing and perceiving and, thus, behaving. This persuasion is vital in creating a truly global market.

The turmoil of financial markets is a confirmation of these ways. There is a constant contrast between global circulation of capitals and the fact that each of the principal actors decide on interest rates and macro-economic policies only on the basis of his or her very short-term interest. Even public opinion responds only to national logics. The attempt to change the policies from top down will never work because the vital push has to come from the bottom up, that is from the market. Only by creating a truly global market, can we then take these decisions at national levels, which are consistent with the globalization process. Therefore, liberalization has to be used as the operating lever on national policies to allow them to respond appropriately to the global needs. To make this liberalization come true, the WTO's 150 members have to be persuaded that it is in their direct interest and that—if they really want it to happen—they have to obey the rules of the multilateral trade/investment game.

Nearly four billion people are moving from central economies to market ones, from poverty to the first stages of production and consumption. This revolution has only one answer: the liberalization of markets which is the engine of global growth. The great victory of the western world over communism has been free trade because it creates interdependence and eliminates, therefore, obstacles among people's mobility, accessibility, and ways of communicating. Protectionism is the opposite and destroys resources, create the basis for nationalisms and violence. If the developing countries are not allowed to export goods, they will export people. And if we try to stop them the alternative will be violence and war. Therefore, the liberalization of trade has not only an economic explanation but it is, above all, the only way to achieve greater international security. To understand this and act accordingly, means to consider the risks, to minimize them, to evaluate and maximize the opportunities.

It has taken more than 30 years of deliberate economic integration for European countries to increase their trade among themselves to 58 per cent of their total trade. In Southeast Asia, where there has been no government intervention and purely as a result of free market forces, intra-regional trade accounts for 63 per cent of the total. But we now live in a global economy requiring a global, transcultural perspective. The 15 different cultures comprising the member states of the European Union, while engaged in shaping a European culture, are ideally placed to co-operate with the emerging Southeast Asian markets, with their hundreds of different cultures.

## PENETRATING INDIVIDUAL MARKETS

European companies aiming to penetrate individual Southeast Asian markets, or to expand their market share in existing markets in Asia in the long term, should consider carefully a number of factors, including the role of cross-cultural communication analysis and strategic alliances.

## The Role of Cross-cultural Communication Analysis

Culture lies at the root of the differences between the various markets in Europe and between individual Asian countries. Our culture conditions our actions and feelings, norms, values, and attitudes; it determines our dietary practices and the type of clothing we wear; and it underlies the way we behave towards others, what we expect of them in return, our perceptions of success and failure, and how we react to and solve problems. Because of the many culturally-determined differences among individuals, it is necessary to consider the role of cross-cultural communication analysis in forging economic partnerships with other cultures. This is a systematic comparison of the similarities and differences in the material and behavioural aspects of all the nations within Europe and Asia. An awareness of the differences thus identified can be used in daily action to better understand the markets and market segments of individual Asian countries, and to develop a strategy for penetrating a particular market that is tailored to the conditions and needs of that culture.

The practical application of cross-cultural communication analysis by a European manager living and working in an Asian country will not eliminate the differences between the two cultures. However, it will help to minimize the detrimental effects of cultural bias in the daily matter of interpreting and accommodating the cultural practices and expectations of one's local colleagues.

## Strategic Alliances

European transnational companies and medium-sized to small companies operating in a united Europe and a transcultural world have looked to strategic alliances as a way of increasing their market share. Views differ on the effectiveness of such alliances in promoting business ventures, although they offer different advantages according to the specific objectives of the companies concerned.

The objective of transnational companies is to systematically maximize foreign market opportunities which are chosen for their potential contribution to the global portfolio. The objective of medium-sized to small companies, on the other hand, is to select opportunities based on their individual potential. In this sense they are more entrepreneurial than transnational companies because they are quick to act on key information which, if used properly, can create a distinct competitive advantage. The advantage of this has not been lost on the transnational companies, which are now restructuring in order to become more like medium-sized and small companies—that is, independent micro-enterprises, with each operating unit pursuing its own strategies but working together with the others when appropriate. There is extensive literature on the many ways of doing business internationally, and we will not consider them further here.

A variety of business tools can be used to conceive, design, and implement strategic policies aimed at maximizing global market share or individual opportunities. One of these is creating customer/supplier networks on a world-wide or local basis, as appropriate, by either conventional or unconventional means. Conventional forms include licensing, managing contracts, turnkey operations, and joint ventures. Less conventional methods include countertrading (an agreement where the sale of goods and services to a country is linked to an obligation to buy from that country) and subcontracting (which links exports of unfinished or semi-finished products to subsequent re-import of the finished goods).

Among the first Asian countries to make extensive use of countertrading was Indonesia. On 2 December 1981, Indonesia faced an imminent shortage of foreign currency when oil revenues plummeted. The government responded by introducing mandatory countertrade requirements in respect of all civil public sector contracts financed by the state budget and by export credits. A 100 per cent counter-purchase obligation was required, and in order to maximize earnings the Indonesians refused to allow exporters to take back their most saleable products, oil and natural gas. Indonesia was joined by Malaysia, which set up a special countertrade unit, while other countries in the region adopted a case-by-case approach.

Subcontracting was first used extensively in Asia by Japan in the late 1960s, when Japanese trading companies set up agreements with local producers in Hong Kong, Taiwan, and Singapore to produce goods mainly for the American market. Among European firms, German manufacturers have been the most active in using Asian subcontractors.

Both the conventional and unconventional forms of doing business discussed above differ from conventional exporting, where the international company's only partner is the foreign distributor or trading company. Within the European Union, collaboration among small firms is being promoted through the Business Cooperation Network (BC-NET), which links up several hundred business advisers throughout the Union to deal with all aspects of the innovation process and promote technology exchange through the Strategic Programme for Information and Technology Transfer (SPRINT). Other programmes which support European research and development include BRITE, ESPRIT, and EUREKA.

Outside the EU, i.e. in Southeast Asia, the EU Commission established three new groups of initiatives: the European Business Information Centers (EBICs)—to provide commercially relevant information and value added services to European and Asian companies—recently opened in Manila, Bangkok, Kuala Lumpur and Jakarta; the Technology Windows in Asia (TWA)—to identify technology suppliers opportunities in Asia for European companies and to support the search for solutions to technological challenges—opened in Singapore and Bangkok; the Support Programme for Economic Cooperation (SPEC) whose task was to survey organizations, in five European and four Asian states views on how Europe should co-operate with Asia.

## CONCLUSION

As European companies grow, they inevitably seek to expand outside geographically determined frontiers and their vision becomes international and/or global. This change affects everyone they deal with, including individuals, other businesses, and governments. The act of sending an expatriate to manage a company's operations in a host country in Asia reflects this change in vision and attitude. What matters most is the capability of meeting Asian expectations—according to the Asian ways of seeing and perceiving; the adaptability to local cultures; the flexibility to switch from one business to another; education, the size and power of the market, being innovative, and having financial and bargaining power; it is irrelevant whether the company is British-based, or French, German, Danish, American, or Japanese. This is a vital consideration in forging what we shall call Europe Inc., which is necessary in order to effectively meet the Asian needs/expectations and compete in the global economy with the United States (USA Inc.) and Japan (Japan Inc.). The concept of European companies redefining themselves along these lines will be discussed later in this book.

It follows from the above that the issues and problems facing a foreign company based in a host country in Southeast Asia are not directly related to its size. Rather, the effectiveness of the expatriate manager in bridging the cultural gap between him or herself and the local partners, managers, employees and government officials will determine the success or failure of the entire operation. Success lies, like the tip of an iceberg, on a firm foundation of cross-cultural communication.

## ENDNOTES

[1]Bank for International Settlements (BIS) 1995.
[2]London *Financial Times*, 27 April 1995, p. 7.

# 2
# The Rationale for a Co-operative Framework

What role can Europe play in the development of a global business framework? Where and when should the initiative be taken? Who is already participating, and why? This chapter considers these "five Ws", and prepares the way for how it can be done: in effect, the subject of this book.

We will consider, first, why Asia and Europe are important to each other and draw some constructive conclusions about the mutual benefits of a co-operative partnership. The chapter then addresses the image each has of the other and the factors that have hindered co-operation in the past. We conclude by examining the process of intra-regional integration and how this has helped to overcome differences within both Europe and Asia, and the lessons that can be learned from this in terms of co-operation between Europe and Asia.

## THE BENEFITS OF CO-OPERATION

### Asia's Importance to Europe

Fifty-nine per cent of the world's population lives in Asia, accounting for 25 per cent of world trade and 27 per cent of world gross national product (GNP). By the end of the century, about 45 per cent of world market growth is expected to be generated in the developing countries of Asia. The highest percentage annual growth rates in Asian countries are up to four or five times those experienced by European countries. By the year 2000, the combined economies of Asia will exceed those of Europe and North America combined, and the region will be home to two-thirds of the world's affluent households (that is, middle-class households with a disposable income of US$30 000 or more).

The area considered here includes the member countries of the Association of South-East Asian Nations (ASEAN)—Brunei, Malaysia, Indonesia, the Philippines, Singapore, Thailand, and the newly admitted (1995) Vietnam—as well as Cambodia, possibly the next to join in 1997. In 1992, total GNP was some US$408 billion, and the total population numbered 453 million.

Singapore, which had the rest of ASEAN as its natural hinterland long before the Association was formalized in 1967, has no natural resources of its own, yet it has experienced an industrialization process which puts it on an equal footing with many European countries. Malaysia and Thailand, as a result of continuous development of their manufacturing bases, have become Newly Industrialized Countries (NICs) with a GNP per capita of around US$3000 and $2000 respectively. Indonesia has initiated a series of bold liberalization measures, including continuous industrialization and the development of such high-tech projects as Asia's first aircraft manufacturing facility, and is rapidly climbing the regional development ladder. The Philippines' economy is recovering from its political troubles and is experiencing skyrocketing growth. Brunei, with a per capita GNP of over US$21 000, is now planning to diversify its economy so as to reduce its heavy dependence on oil exports. The highest rate of growth among the ASEAN countries, however, has occurred in Vietnam as a result of foreign investment.

In order to sustain their economic development, Asian governments are investing heavily in telecommunications networks. Despite its having more than half of the world's population, Asia (excluding Japan) has only around 10 per cent of its telephone lines. In China, India, Indonesia, and Vietnam, there is less than one phone line per 100 people. However, INDOSAT (Indonesia's first international privatization) aims to install 5 million new telephone lines by 1999. Currently, the 190 million Indonesians are served by just 2.2 million lines. Over the next 10 years, the Indonesian region will need in excess of US$160 billion in infrastructure. A commitment has also been made to develop power-generation facilities. Within the next 10 years, 180 gigawatts (GW, or thousands of megawatts) of new power capacity will be needed in Asia, producing a predicted 7 per cent growth in this sector. By the year 2000, a dozen new international airports will be in operation in Asia, with others planned or under construction. The list of infrastructure projects includes roads, railway networks, and more. The total estimated bill for this infrastructure push, which is aimed at sustaining the present economic renaissance, is US$3 trillion.

Of course, stages of development and rates of growth vary throughout the region. Over the past three decades, some countries have performed exceptionally, even miraculously, well; others have taken significant strides and a number have yet to catch up. For this reason, the countries in the region have variously been described as soaring eagles, high-flying geese, and, in a few cases, lame ducks!

Despite the varying stages of development of individual countries, it is apparent that Asia has a dynamic and vibrant economic future. There is a growing interdependence among the Asian nations, and they are becoming increasingly interested in trading among themselves. Intra-regional investment now accounts for about 40 per cent of Asia's total foreign direct investment (FDI). The region might even be called a powerhouse of job creation. When Exxon Corporation signed an agreement with Indonesia in November 1994 to proceed with the world's largest offshore gas development project, at a cost of US$40 billion, US President Clinton stated, "If America is vigorous and effective in Asia over the next decade, Asia could add more than 1.8 million jobs to the American economy."

Sixty per cent of the inflow of foreign direct investment into developing countries goes to Asia. For many decades, the pattern was for colonial powers to invest in their existing and former colonies. This is now changing as a result of three factors: the increasing role being played by the NICs; the actions of regional governments to reduce the amount of red tape and improve the environment for foreign investment; and changing conditions in other parts of the world.

Asia plays a leading role in the world's financial markets, which could be used by European companies in setting up joint ventures in Asia. Asian central banks hold more than one-third of the world's foreign exchange reserves. Asia's indebtedness is one of the lowest in the world and is far lower than that of Latin America.

The world's fastest-growing air cargo routes are intra-Asian routes, together with those linking Pacific Asia with Europe and North America. The major air corridor of Singapore–Bangkok–Taipei–Tokyo is the region's economic axis. Seventy per cent of the world's jumbo jets are occupied on trans-Pacific routes, and the average yearly passenger traffic increase in Asia is 9 per cent, as against the 5 per cent world average. This air traffic growth is creating not only new types of aircraft, but also strategic alliances and stiff competition. The new 777 jet developed by Boeing, which came into operation—in Cathay Pacific's fleet—in 1996 has been specifically designed to meet Asian needs. The co-operation between airlines in the region, and the creation of new international linkages, is resulting in the formation of a number of strategic alliances. For example, the Thai Airlines–Lufthansa–United Airlines alliance has become the largest international air services network. And there is competition between Singapore's Changi and Bangkok's Don Muang airports to become the premier hub in the region.

The "Singapore Girl" of the Singapore Airlines' advertising campaign symbolizes the rapid growth in air travel in the region. Over the years of the campaign, the "Singapore Girl" image has been transformed from a symbol of Singaporean life to one of Asian dynamism, affluence, and influence. The image now encompasses the different cultures in the countries serviced by the airline also because the recruitment of the "Singapore Girl" now spans from Singapore to Malaysia and Indonesia and mirrors, in a sense, the transformation of Southeast Asia itself from the region which sparked the domino theory at the time of the Vietnam War to today's economic dynamo.

The growth of intermodalism is increasingly becoming indispensable, not only to Hong Kong, Japan, and Taiwan but also to the entire region's major container ports. For example, in Tanjung Priok, in Jakarta, Indonesia, container movements grew by 34 per cent in 1994 alone. Every four minutes a ship enters Singapore's port, the busiest in Asia. Port Klang, near Kuala Lumpur, the capital of Malaysia, is investing US$593 million in infrastructure development in order to manage the ever-increasing volume of traffic. And the world's second-largest operator of container ships, the Taiwanese conglomerate Evergreen, is investing US$1 billion in developing the port of Batam Island in Indonesia.

The future of Asia lies in its new geometrical configurations. For example, the SMIT (Singapore–Malaysia–Indonesia) triangle links Singapore to the state of Johore (Malaysia) and the Indonesian provinces of Riau, Batam Island, and the Buitan and Bulu Islands. A further example is the East Asian Growth Area (EAGA) founded in 1994, its headquarters secretariat is in Brunei and includes the east Malaysian states of Sarawak and Sabah, the southern Philippines islands of Mindanao and the Indonesian islands of Kalimantan, Sulawesi and Maluku. However, the Philippines represents — with Subic Bay free port and Clark Air Force Base, both former US naval and air force bases, as well as other facilities — a potential growth area in itself.

Asia is vitally important to Europe for two additional, and crucial, reasons. Asians know more about Europe than Europeans know (beyond their exotic vacations) about Asia. Europeans would do well to imitate the quest for information evidenced in Asia. There is also abundant evidence of what might be called a booming confidence among Asians in the prospects for the region. When the typically cautious European business person goes to Asia, this booming confidence is evident all around, not least in the newest generation of skyscrapers that speak of power, wealth, and corporate megafirms. The Jim Mao Building in Shanghai (1380 ft, or 420 m high), will be completed in 1997, one year after the even higher Petronas Tower in Kuala Lumpur, which itself will be dwarfed by the Chongquing Tower 1500 ft high in southwest China, due for completion in 1998 epitomizing the economic boom in China. The new millennium will be marked by the 2625 ft (800 m) Millennium Tower in Japan, 1172 ft (357 m) higher than the Sears Tower in Chicago; and in 2004, Taiwan will have Asia Plaza in Kaohsiung.

This symbolic expression of soaring confidence finds a horizontal form in Vietnam with the planned transformation of Saigon from a dilapidated city at the end of the Vietnam War into a 21st century international business centre without rival in the region. It will comprise 2600 hectares of science parks, universities, a business and financial centre, shopping centres, warehouses, and office blocks linked by an ultramodern ring road to the airport.

A final expression of the booming confidence in Asia is the mobility of the people. According to the World Travel and Tourism Council in Brussels, the Pacific–Asia region's total annual tourism output will increase from US$800 billion in 1995 to US$2 trillion in 2005.

Given all of the above, one might easily assume that European businesses are falling over themselves in their haste to participate in the dynamic growth of the Asian region. However, there is little evidence of this. In terms of financial flows, the European record is unsatisfactory. In 1994, for example, Asia received US$52 billion of foreign direct investment, or little more than a quarter of the world total and only about US$5 billion more than in 1993. European countries have paid less attention to Asia than have other industrialized nations. Between 1980 and 1993, European Union-based companies invested an average of US$2.2 billion annually in Asia, compared with US$4.2 billion invested by US companies and US$3.4 billion by Japan. (A bird's-eye view of the importance of Southeast Asia to Europe is included in Appendix No. 1.)

As every action implies an opposite reaction; how is Europe responding to Asia's booming confidence? With a booming uncertainty?

### Europe's Importance to Asia

The answer to the question of why Europe is important to Asia can be found only through an awareness of Asia's needs and how Europe can meet them. Asia needs Europe in order to be able to exert its economic independence. There is widespread concern in Asia, for example, that science and technology professionals may become too dependent on Japan/USA Inc. as suppliers of capital goods, investment, and technology. Thus, Asian officials and business executives are actively seeking the presence of European professionals in the region in order to speed up the growth process. Europe has been slow to respond in this respect. But it has not been in the sales of weapons.

Defence spending in Southeast Asia is significant. In 1994 alone a total of US$13.9 billion has been spent in the region (i.e. Thailand US$3.4 billion; Singapore US$3.0 billion; Malaysia US$2.7 billion; Indonesia US$2.3 billion; Vietnam US$0.9 billion; Cambodia US$0.1 billion; Laos US$0.1 billion). This year American weapons sales declined, as in the previous four years. This was because Asian buyers saw in Europe the chance to avoid becoming dependent on American suppliers in case the USA cuts back future arms sales. Furthermore, they were also attracted by lower prices, and equipment—like submarines—that the USA does not sell. Thus, arms sales by Britain, France, Germany and Italy alone increased by 30 per cent over the 1990–4 period. One reason for this slow response is that it hasn't yet achieved a single, united voice with which to convince Asian entrepreneurs of their collective interest and ability to back up words with deeds. A second reason is that European Union budgetary allocations have long emphasized development rather than economic co-operation. Another reason is the vast majority of European executives and entrepreneurs prefer to take a short-term—rather than a long-term—view of economic performance in Asia. That is, they prefer export arrangements to joint ventures, and to compete with one another over Asian markets, than to forge strategic alliances in Europe and then compete successfully against their global competitors in securing contracts in Asia.

Finally, the reason why Asia needs Europe lies in its need to master conflict resolution through co-operation. European economic assistance could also, indirectly, assist Asia in meeting its security needs. In order to eliminate conflicts, Asia must accelerate its non-institutionalized process of regional integration, achieve practical results with its own version of the G7 summit, APEC, and set down roots for its Seattle, USA, Bogor, Indonesia, Osaka, Japan and Manila, Philippines 1996 agreements on its "free trade" vision. Europe could then make a unique contribution in furthering global advancement towards free trade.

Asia also needs Europe in order to keep up the pace of human resources development and the technological transfer needed to transform its industries from labour-intensive to capital-intensive manufacturing. Malaysia, for example, has become impatient at the slow pace of technology transfer by Japan and has invited Europe to take its place.

Many countries in Asia benefit from both bilateral (that is, nation-to-nation) and multilateral (that is, European Union) assistance. Between 1976 and 1991, assistance from the European Union to the ASEAN countries totalled US$6.97 billion (compared with US$17.2 billion from Japan and US$3.7 billion from the United States), while Vietnam received US$642.6 million (Japan US$131.5 million and the United States $70 million).

The existing instruments for Europe's institutionalized industrial and economic co-operation with Asia include—in addition to those mentioned at the end of Chapter One—an array of instruments such as European Investment Bank loans, European Investment Partners programmes, European Business Councils, and generalized systems of trade preferences or GSP (which provide European Union markets with access to some 72 per cent of Asian imports). Two-way trade between Europe and emerging Asia reached US$212 billion at the end of 1994. In 1988–94 this volume of trade more than doubled and it grew faster than its trade with Eastern Europe.

The story these figures tell is that Europe (that is, the European Union institutions and the individual member states with their bilateral co-operation agreements) is the third largest trading partner of, and the second principal source of official development assistance to, the ASEAN nations. Further institutionalized developments in the coming years will be determined by the new momentum of co-operation begun at the Asem or the European Union–Asia summit of March 1996 in Bangkok. The Asia–Europe Meeting, Asem, as it has become known, was attended by the seven ASEAN member states (Brunei, Indonesia, Malaysia, Philippines, Singapore, Thailand, and Vietnam), representatives of Japan, South Korea and China as well as the 15 European Union heads of government together with the EU officials.

The importance to fill in the missing link in the global strategic network of linkages between the world's major centres of economic gravity was first floated 16 months before by Singapore Prime Minister Goh Chok Tong. Asia and America have come together through APEC, Europe and America have a relationship dating back to the 1950s with NATO and are now thinking of creating the Transatlantic Free Trade Area (TAFTA). With the sole exception of ASEAN–EU institutionalized dialogues, Europe and Asia do not have solid bridges linking them. Therefore, the Bangkok meeting set the stage for creating just that missing link that will uphold the new world order under the WTO ruling. In this sense the fact that Asem took place, such a short time after the original idea was voiced, was in itself an historic achievement.

During the planning stage, Asem's aim was to lay the groundwork to negotiate long lasting investment, security and politics to fill the vacuum in the global network of linkages.

During the summit, Asem's host, Thailand Prime Minister Banharn Silpa-archa called on Europe to tap into Asia's economic dynamism in return for Europe's wealth of experience, expertise and technology—in a spirit of equal partnership and mutual respect. At the end of the summit, he declared that Asem had "achieved more than we expected". He was echoed by the EU Commission's President Jacques Santer who stated "it is an historic turning point in our relations".

This achievement was seen to be the beginning of a process, envisaging within the 1996–8 period five new initiatives. First, the creation of a Joint Government and Private Sector Working Group to set the direction and tone for the new relationship. It will have to draw up an Asia–Europe Investment Promotion Action Plan (IPAP) by September 1996.

Asem's second achievement was the creation of a Euro-Asia Business Forum and an on-line Euro-Asia training and technology exchange to promote inter-regional co-operation. It will hold its first meeting in France at the end of 1996. Acknowledging that French companies are underperforming in Asia (even though the number of companies present in Singapore rose in the last 10 years, from 100 to 400, and that France accounts for only 2 per cent of Asia trade) lecturing at the Singapore Institute of Southeast Asian Studies, French President Jacques Chirac stated "without trying to hide inevitable divergences of interest, we should highlight the fact that we represent for each other the most promising markets. Let us have the courage to eliminate progressively obstacles to trade in the framework of an open regionalism that guarantee our prosperity." Then, he informally floated the idea of such a Business Forum. It was then officially proposed in Bangkok.

Asem's third achievement was the creation of an Asia–Europe Foundation, to be based in Singapore, to promote East–West academic and cultural exchanges, to which the government of Singapore pledged US$1m.

The fourth agreed measure was that Malaysia will co-ordinate a study to integrate Asia's and Europe's railway networks and the creation of a new Europe–Asia Environmental Technology Center (EAETC).

The final approved measure was directly related to how to continue the dialogue. It envisaged: a July 1996 meeting in Brussels among senior officials to discuss new ways to promote trade and investment; a 1997 meeting in Japan of economic ministers to discuss relevant economic issues; a meeting of Asian and EU foreign ministers to be held in Singapore in 1997 and a second Asem summit in London in 1998.

Commenting on Asem, the Director-General of the WTO, Ambassador Renato Ruggiero stated:

> "Europe has to be ready to match the kind of market-opening measures already agreed as targets by Asia and the USA. Whatever the short-term costs, the opportunity for Europe to open its markets in order to have Asian markets completely open is much greater than the risk. I really hope European government leaders came back from the Asem with the full awareness that in Asia this is an historical moment. The USA and Asian countries have already settled on their goal, a full trade area that would cover fifty per cent of world trade by the year 2020. Now Europe has to be ready to match this goal."[1]

According to the 1996 report by Australia's Industry Commission the incremental gains which would be generated after APEC's 2020 measures have been worked through have been estimated as US$303 billion per annum for its members.

Although at the Asem there was a distinct fear among Asian nations that Europe could be a "free rider" in this new relationship (without market opening measures of its own, regardless of the outcome of the 1996 APEC meeting). Because of Europe's new attitude towards Asia, it could very well be that Europe will take these kind of measures precisely to demonstrate to Asia that it is a partner on an equal basis, it does not need to fear, it is factually respected and that Europe has indeed changed its attitude towards Asia for good. Hence it is very serious towards Asia.

The strength of these fears and the soundness of this new European attitude are going to be tested when the Working

Group will review the Asian and European approaches to the actual development of investment promotion action programme. The Asian approach seems to aim at studying six economic areas: review two-way investment between Asia and Europe, identify barriers to investment, identify protective investment sectors, matching European–Asian investment partners for other regions like Indochina, South Asia and/or Eastern Europe; establishing financial networks to mobilize projects and the study of investment related issues such as labour standards, technology transfer and the environment. The European approach results from the 1994 EU Commission Communication *Towards a New Strategy for Asia* where priorities (such as strengthening Europe's profile and economic presence in Asia, the promotion of mutual awareness and understanding, increased access of medium and small companies on business opportunities, and the facilitation of business linkages and investment opportunities) were clearly set. Asians are afraid that Europe aims at securing an investment code binding Asia to set rules to prise open Asian markets and to provide guarantees on difficult questions such as repatriation of profits and nationalization. Fearing a possible loss of total control of how foreign investments should operate within their countries, they are concerned. However, both approaches will be before the established Working Group whose sole purpose is to prepare an action plan to be submitted to the 27 leaders for approval. Afterwards it will be presented at the WTO First Council Meeting to be held in December 1996 in Singapore.

APEC and Asem could indeed effectively become two separate parts of one continuous multilateral discussion including not only comprehensive sets of rules for foreign trade but also for foreign direct investment because the two are critically linked. About a third of all world trade takes place between affiliates of businesses located in different countries posing different barriers to investment. To break down these barriers, opening up markets to foreign trade, provide consistency, clarity and predictability for investors, and guard against protectionism, a Multilateral Investment Agreement (MIA) has been widely advocated by businessmen as part and parcel of the global investment and competition policy rules to be considered within the WTO.

This new combined APEC/Asem attitude would mean profound changes for businesses because both will make it easier for European and Asian companies to use Asia and Europe regions as operating bases.

As the focus of this book is the presence, both individually and collectively, of transnational and medium-sized to small companies in the Southeast Asian markets, there will be no further consideration of official and institutionalized relations between Europe and Southeast Asia.

## Conclusion

The benefits of a co-operative partnership between Europe and Asia are such that the two parties might effectively build a relationship that would unite them in dealing with the problem of global competition—that is, Japan Inc. and USA Inc. versus Europe Inc. Europe can play a vital role in this process. The role of the governments is to facilitate this process and to give the political support for a broader and deeper economic constructive engagement between the two regions. Furthermore, if European companies are able to position themselves in terms of the development of the Southeast Asian markets, they will be well placed to take a role in the continued economic development of India and China.

The bird's-eye view presented here indicates that in developing a co-operative business relationship, the benefits to European transnational and medium-sized to small companies of investing in Asian markets will derive not so much from those companies' knowledge of the array of investment incentives and legislation favouring foreign investment in those countries as from their ability to create a new momentum, a net impetus of technology and skills and access to international markets. In order to achieve this ultimate objective, it is essential that cultural barriers be overcome through a process of adaptation. Without adaptation, and the participation in development that can evolve from it, there can be no real sharing of know-how, since information networks and knowledge are valued more highly than entrepreneurial spirit in Asia.

Prospective customers might be encouraged to visit Western Europe in order to gauge for themselves the combined strengths of Europe's indigenous suppliers. Many of these prospective customers are generally aware of the technology available from Europe, although they will not necessarily be fully aware of the latest relevant developments. Of paramount importance is a vision and sound organization and financial engineering to sustain it. The availability of competitive (that is, compared with Japan and the United States) finance, is a prerequisite to business success in Asia. More and more of this finance will be required by the private sector as the process of privatization gathers pace. The provision of private sector finance could be a key factor in Europe gaining a head-start in Asia, if Europe Inc. can rise to the challenge.

The role which the European construction industry might play in Asia is a case in point. By around 2010 the estimated total value of construction development in Asia is US$3 trillion. At present, the Japanese are snapping up the construction contracts, while the United States contributes advice, design, and project management. European businesses are encouraged to participate in the bidding for contracts, because of the Asian preference for three-way competition, but they are unable to compete as equals with their global rivals due to their lack of unity. The end-result of this situation is that European contractors are being left with the crumbs of the contract pie. If Europe wants to be considered competitive enough to win a sizeable share of the market, it needs to project a united image.

Most European companies have yet to appreciate the pace of Asia's regional economic integration, backed by the impressive and growing affluence of its consumers, and its growing influence in world affairs. There are some exceptions, however. In the 1994 fiscal year, Siemens, the German electrical group, received Asian orders totalling DM 12 billion (US$8.11 billion), compared with DM 2.5 billion (US$1.8 billion) in orders by Eastern Europe. Its investment of DM 1.5 billion (US$1.09 billion) in Asia in 1994 is planned to increase to DM 5 billion (US$3.63 billion) by the year 2000. In 1995, Siemens held a board meeting in Singapore, the first held outside of Germany. In 1995 Daimler Benz concluded a deal to assemble Mercedes Benz cars in India and Vietnam, and another (worth US$2.5 billion) with China's Aviation Industry General Corporation to develop a new jet plane carrying 100–120 passengers. Volkswagen exports Audi cars to China, and Peugeot is planning two plants in China. Imperial Chemical Industries (ICI), the giant British pharmaceuticals group, earns more than half of its profits in Southeast Asian markets.

France, Germany, the Netherlands, and the United Kingdom account for some 90 per cent of the European Union's direct investments in Asian markets, according to the UN Conference on Trade and Development. Their combined outlays in the region more than tripled between 1980 and 1993, rising from US$7.4 billion to US$26.1 billion. However, Europe still lags behind Japan and the United States. By the end of 1993, Japanese and US investment in the region totalled US$30.8 billion and US$39.4 billion respectively, or an annual average of US$4.2 billion and US$2.4 billion respectively, compared with an annual average figure for European investors of US$2.2 billion. In other words, between 1980 and 1993 Japanese investments in Asia grew by 650 per cent, US investments by 460 per cent, and European investments by a comparatively low 350 per cent. Furthermore, German companies' stock of foreign direct investment in the region was only half that of their investments in Spain. The Asian assets of French companies equalled their assets in Ireland, while the value of British companies' investments was similar to that of their interests in Australia. This picture of European lethargy in investing in Asia is counterbalanced by a World Bank study showing

> "that between 1986 and 1992 the countries of the EU and the United States invested roughly equal emounts in Asia. European investment in Asia began to grow rapidly in the late 1980s. In 1992, European investment in South East Asia increased by 87% while Japanese

investments increased by just 12% according to the Japanese official figures. What both the UN and the World Bank reports show is that both America and Europe are small investors compared with the Asians themselves."[2]

Thus the potential for increased participation of European businesses in the powerhouse of growth that is Asia today is obvious, and would go a long way towards reducing the unemployment figure of around 20 million.

At the forefront of the move to raise the profile of Europe in Asia has been Germany's Chancellor Kohl, who visited the region in 1993. In addition to securing contracts worth US$4 billion, Kohl began the process of creating a concerted European effort in Asia based on co-operation rather than confrontation. This new course was stated in the Essen EU 94 Summit Declaration, which welcomed a position paper prepared by the EU Commission outlining Europe's inability to compete world-wide if it failed to forge close ties with Asia. It also urged the EU Council of Ministers and the Commission to report on all practical measures to raise Europe's profile in Asia, and tacitly endorsed the Singapore Prime Minister's call for the first Asem summit held in Bangkok, 1–2 March 1996.

While the above might attest to European commitment to Asia today, it is no guarantee that Europe will be able to transform potential customers in Asia into actual customers. Let us consider an example. Many Asian business leaders and government officials know only about Japanese specifications, machinery, software and other essential products. This is due not to the unavailability of equivalent European products, but rather to the investment Japan Inc. has made in training its potential customers to think Japanese. This "training" was done with little fanfare by marketing professionals based in the representative offices of Japanese companies throughout the region. Although business leaders, government officials, and entrepreneurs in those host countries were also potential European customers, they were unaware of what Europe had to offer because they weren't approached systematically and regularly by European marketeers in the way they had been courted by the Japanese. They weren't transformed from potential customers into actual customers, because the majority of European companies considered the cost of such a patient courtship prohibitive. A further reason might be the lack, among European companies, of capillary organizational skills known as organizational engineering. Finally, because Japan Inc. was able to turn potential customers into actual customers over the long term, its customers are likely to remain faithful to the relationship. In other words, they had started thinking Japanese.

Another elucidating example is joint venture agreements. For every 10 successfully concluded Japanese investment applications in the Southeast Asian region, there are only two successful American ventures and one European. Many expatriate managers representing their companies in the Asian markets are focused primarily on clinching deals. Once the contract is signed, they can go home to a fat bonus and leave the problem-solving to others. However, the company representatives who are responsible for "nursing the baby" may lack the Asian patience required to adhere to procedures and deal with government bureaucracy. This problem is essentially a cross-cultural one stemming from inadequate or inappropriate training of the European representatives, and a lack of motivation and understanding of the local culture. A further reason for the lack of success of many joint ventures is the failure to fully involve the local partner as a true equal. This is often manifested in disregard for local business practices and attempts to bypass the accepted channels and procedures. A basic difference between European and Asian approaches to setting up a joint venture is the role played by the negotiator of the contract. Asian partners prefer to see the same person carry on the relationship as the resident manager of the joint venture, whereas European companies prefer to withdraw the key person once the deal is signed and send someone else, who is unknown to the local partners, to fill this role. In short, for Asian business partners, the relationship is all-important. By disregarding this, European businesses are undermining the foundations of any venture conducted with Asian partners. They have to realise in Southeast Asian markets they do not negotiate a contract, but a long-term relationship.

This is where the Japanese have shown their commitment and, in the process, secured the lion's share of the market. Their long-term investment of time and financial resources has turned potential partners into actual partners. European companies need to make a similar long-term investment if they are to reap the long-term profits. In other words, they need to put their organizational engineering house in order.

## FACTORS INHIBITING CO-OPERATION

The bulk of European industry is comprised of medium-sized and small companies. The same is true of industry in Southeast Asia. Such companies can only expand by conquering new markets and incorporating new technologies. However, they may be unsure of how to go about doing this, or fearful of what it entails, unlike transnational companies. These shared fears at the organizational level are compounded by the fears that both Europe and Southeast Asia have experienced in developing their institutionalized relationship.

We will now consider how the image that Asia and Europe have of each other has inhibited economic co-operation in the past.

### Europe's Image Problem in Asia

Europe is feared by Asia for a variety of reasons, ranging from its reputation as a politically inept and inward-looking "fortress", to its lack of a vision or strategy for its involvement with Asia and the resulting perception in Asia that Europe Inc. lacks a united presence in the region. "When I was a child," said one Malaysian businessman, "I used to see only European products. Now I see only Japanese know-how." This perceived lack of assertive presence has created fears that Europe could never really understand Asia as a trusted partner on an equal basis. It is only by being immersed in a culture that one can identify the actual needs of those markets. Once they have been understood, then it is possible to shape a response that is specifically designed to satisfy them as they actually are in Southeast Asia, not as Europeans would like them to be from Europe.

A widespread perception in Asia is that Europeans are unable to shape events and are evasive in reacting to them, inflexible in matters of democracy and human rights, and concerned more with fashionable, rather than long-term, issues. Europeans are perceived as talkers, not doers. Theirs is seen as a play-safe culture focused on taking short-term bites in the form of increased exports from Asia, rather than a long-term commitment in the form of increased investment. Unaccustomed to official meetings held in informal camaraderie, to create consensus, Europeans restrict themselves to formal agendas and timetables, searching for breakthroughs and winners and losers at the negotiating table; working to keep, not to dismantle, "Fortress-Europe"; talking about a common currency which is, to their ways of seeing and perceiving, a farce; clinging to the past of its obsolete ideas; unable to learn from Asian miracles—in which an ability to learn quickly, adopt it and adapt to one's own situation played a significant part. They seem to be unable to learn because they do not really know Asia. Thus, they have a one-dimensional view of it, generating a condescending, indifferent, opportunistic and cynical attitude. While Asians see themselves as knowing Europe much better than Europeans know Asia. Some Europeans see themselves as representatives of a superior civilization. The Deputy Prime Minister of Malaysia, Mr Anwar Ibrahim voiced his widespread feeling in Southeast Asia when he stated "Asians are no longer willing to be lectured and hectored by those who consider that they still have a civilising mission in Asia".[3]

Yet, Europeans seem to be awash in pessimism freezing them into inaction—unlike the much admired "can do" American attitude—and thus generate a welfare state, which is out of control, high unemployment and low growth.

Perhaps the ultimate fallout of the March 1996 Bangkok summit will be the mustering of that new EU's will allowing Europe to enhance its image in Asia as a doer not a talker. Such a change implies responsibilities to be shared across a wide spectrum of players within Europe. From an Asian perspective this change of attitude can be demonstrated in substance in several ways among which they consider the following: opening up the EU markets to the Asians; not trying to impose European labour standards on poorer societies in Asia; leading with the Americans the development of the World Trading System under WTO ruling, rather than following the USA.

Other potential problems are the image Europe has of prioritizing Latin American and Mediterranean countries over Asia. There is some concern that with increasing competition for limited resources, Europe will adopt an increasingly standardized form of economic and development co-operation without making allowances for qualitative cultural differences—a kind of "on-tap" standard supply. This also works in reverse:

> "[The] fear that the EU is roller-coasting people's identity into oblivion must be treated with the utmost seriousness, however unfocused much of the criticism may be. For it is on our handling of this question above all others that future generations will judge the European Union."[4]

Asians are also concerned about European businesses' failure to make full use of local capabilities in Asia, which can be more responsive to local attitudes, as well as more economical and cost-effective. Finally, they fear that when programmes and projects co-financed by Europe are handled by the World Bank or the Asian Development Bank, Europe loses its identity. The lack of transparency of European institutions creates complicated and confusing procedures and long delays.

In addition to the various fears discussed above, Asian business leaders, government officials, and entrepreneurs have complained that co-operation between Europe and Asia in the areas of science and technology has been seriously hampered by a lack of funds, especially when compared with the funds earmarked for co-operation in this field by Japan Inc. and USA Inc. Little effort has been made to find appropriate "niches" where co-operation would be mutually beneficial in the long term, as has been the case with Japan and the United States. European companies aren't given financial incentives in the way that Japanese companies are, even though such incentives would help to secure a position in the markets of Southeast Asia that would ultimately lead to successful industrial and technological co-operation. Europe lacks the vision to consider the countries of

Southeast Asia as a strategic bridgehead in the global struggle against Japan Inc. and USA Inc. European companies are unable to seize business opportunities in Southeast Asian markets quickly enough — that is, at the speed with which those markets operate. This is seen to stem largely from the prevailing sense of disunity in Europe, which makes it difficult for companies and institutions to effectively co-ordinate their efforts at competing for markets. Other reasons are the inability of European businesses to gain an adequate intelligence/information-gathering advantage over their non-European competitors, their delay in reacting to business leads and general uncertainty, their lack of willingness to share information with their competitors and other institutions and organizations in Europe, and their inability to effectively monitor the business climate on a continuous basis, which creates goodwill and facilitates the performance of Europe's representatives.

The list of complaints goes on. European companies seem to be unaware of, or unable to exploit, the widespread antipathy in Southeast Asia to Japan and the United States and turn it into an effective competitive advantage for Europe. Similarly, they underestimate the many cultural similarities between Europe and many Southeast Asian countries, especially when compared with the United States, and are therefore unable to transform them into a critical competitive advantage. Furthermore, European companies have not adapted their investment strategies to suit local Asian environments. When embarking on any initiative, European companies — unlike their Japanese and American counterparts — do not consult all the institutions involved. As the institutional frameworks in Asian countries are complex, with different departments having areas of overlapping responsibility, it requires time and patience to secure their involvement in the development of new projects. Finally, the dissatisfaction in Asia with Japan Inc. and USA Inc. with regard to technology transfer has not necessarily advantaged European companies, largely because they have shown an unwillingness in the past to take adequate note of local aspirations with regard to the transfer of "core" technology and its eventual assimilation.

## Asia's Image Problem in Europe

For many Europeans living in Europe, Asia is seen only as an exotic vacation destination. The lack of widespread and learned public opinions about Asia partly explains the absence of an effective private business lobby which could help in shaping concerted action by Europe Inc. in Asia. However, various fears also account for the lack of a co-operative partnership with Asian countries. Rising unemployment (now at around 20 million), a recession, and indications that many workers who were laid off during the downturn may lose their jobs permanently, have fuelled fears, voiced by the media, politicians, and business leaders, of the threat to Western Europe from Third World countries—in particular, Southeast Asia. The media have called for greater protection of European industries (and jobs) through import tariffs or quota arrangements. They eloquently argue their case by stating that European enterprises are no match for the competition from Southeast Asia, which has no social security system, no environmental and safety protection, and no respect for intellectual property, and thus no associated costs for industry. Southeast Asia is, quite simply, being blamed for taking jobs away from Europe. It is not taken into account, for example, that an increase in output in poor countries results in an increased output in rich countries, exporting more to developing countries which can afford to import more.

Another fear often mentioned by European companies in Europe is the loss, through legal and/or illegal means, of technology to predatory Asian companies when Europeans go there. Since these predatory companies are notoriously pirates of European technology, protection of foreign technical and business know-how by enforceable law should be in place in those countries in Southeast Asia European companies target. But it is not just a matter of adequate copyright legislation. It is also a matter of effectively enforcing it. In fact, without adequate policing, the European companies' willingness to invest in areas of high technology to create new products in the targeted Southeast Asian country will be dramatically undermined.

### Conclusion

The factors, and fears, outlined above must all be taken into account if European businesses are to assume a more assertive role in Asia generally, as well as in specific Southeast Asian markets. This assertiveness is dependent upon a change of attitude and behaviour, which derives from a learning culture and confidence in who we are, rather than fear of what we are not. The following section on intra-regional and inter-regional integration illustrates how a number of countries have been able to bring about positive changes in this area.

## INTRA-REGIONAL AND INTER-REGIONAL INTEGRATION

Within the span of a few decades, Malaysia has moved from confrontation with China to collaboration. This radical change in its attitude was caused by the bursting of the fear bubble. With 35 per cent of its population Chinese, the Malaysian authorities were concerned about the potentially tumultuous influence of China on its racially integrated society, where Chinese, Indians, Malays, and foreigners live peacefully together. Any turmoil generated as a result of this influence would have produced cracks in the affluence Malaysia was fast acquiring as a result of its socio-economic development programmes. When China adopted its open-door policy in the late 1970s, it was a logical step for Malaysian-Chinese to invest heavily in China's development by securing contracts. Business took the lead, and government and official policies followed. And far from trying to export communism to Malaysia or to lay claim to the disputed Spratlys islands, China opted to invest in Malaysia's dynamic growth. Thus, today there is not only a healthy two-way investment flow between the two countries, but they are also supporting each other in forging the "Asia for Asians" policy which is being crystallized in the East Asia Economic Caucus (EAEC)—or the battleground, as they perceive it, between the developed and the developing worlds.

Asians perceive that the West is afraid of Asia's dynamic growth and believe that it will attempt to block its increasing influence in world affairs. They cite the willingness of Europe and the United States to drive the engine of the World Trade Organization (WTO) in order to slow down the Asian bullet-train, and the West's continued meddling in matters of the environment and human rights, as evidence of this fear. Thus, when the WTO set up its machinery in January 1995, as feverish negotiations went on around world capitals to elect the first Director-General of the WTO, much effort went into trying to ensure that the Chairman of the General Council (the main political body) was an Asian and that the venue of its first ministerial conference would be in Asia. They succeeded on both counts: the Chairman elected was K. Kesavapany, Singapore's Ambassador to Geneva, and the venue was Singapore.

Of the European nations, Germany has made considerable headway in overcoming the fears of local businesses that they would lose out to their Asian competitors. Chancellor Helmut Kohl visited China and Southeast Asia in the autumn of 1993. In *Die Welt*, on 26 September, in an article entitled "The Federal Government's New Far East Concept: active policy to safeguard the industrial location of Germany", Kohl argued the case for an active German policy on Asia. This statement was made by a head of state whose country exports 10 per cent of its world-wide exports to Asia, while Asian imports amount to 15 per cent. Asia is the largest recipient of German foreign investments in the Third World, followed by Latin America. Before Kohl's 1993 visit to Asia, however, it accounted for only 5 per cent of Germany's foreign investments.

In January 1994, the presidency of the European Union went to Greece, but in June of that year it passed to Germany. It is possible, therefore, that German policy on Asia will lead the other 14 EU member states into developing the much-needed common European policy on Asia. The effective implementation of such a policy rests ultimately on the sound management of joint ventures among EU member states, among European businesses, and between the European Union and ASEAN.

In April 1994, Prime Minister Edouard Balladur of France made an extensive trip to Asia. This was another concrete step towards developing France's policy towards Asia. In December 1994, the EU Essen summit issued a communiqué which made three important points. It welcomed the new position paper prepared by the EU Commission which drew attention to Europe's inability to compete world-wide if it failed to forge closer ties between Europe and Asia. It urged the EU Council of Ministers and the Commission to report on all practical measures to raise Europe's profile in Asia, and it tacitly endorsed the Singapore Prime Minister's call for a summit.

These developments took place against the background of other international developments such as ASEAN, NAFTA, and APEC. On 17 November 1993, the US House of Representatives approved the North American Free Trade Agreement (NAFTA). At stake was the economic security of the United States and Canada (by creating jobs, increasing productivity, and raising incomes) in particular, and, in general, regional free trade (that is, the voluntary exploitation of local trading opportunities) and economic geography (that is, transport and transaction costs, and proximity matters in trade).

Between 18 and 20 November 1993, the APEC summit was held in Seattle, in the United States. APEC (Asia–Pacific Economic Cooperation Forum) is an association of Australia, Brunei, Canada, Chile, China, Hong Kong, Indonesia, Japan, Malaysia, Mexico, New Zealand, Papua New Guinea, the Philippines, Singapore, South Korea, Taiwan, Thailand, and the United States, with a per capita income ranging from US$30 000 (Japan) to US$1000 (Indonesia). APEC members make up a region that includes half of the world economy. Today there is no consensus on the purpose of APEC. At one extreme are those nations who dream of creating a free trade zone able to transform the Pacific Rim from a geographical entity into the world's largest free trade area, while at the other extreme are those nations which question its very existence. Japan is concerned that it is a prelude to an Asia–Pacific economic bloc. China sees it as a useful public relations exercise for improving its relationship with the United States and protecting its Most Favoured Nation (MFN) trading status. Thailand regards APEC as too small (and too institutionally underdeveloped) to work outside WTO, yet as too large for a regional agreement on tariff-cutting measures.

Many of the Southeast Asian countries worry that, as minor powers, they risk finding their concerns squeezed out by the United States, Japan, and China—the giants at the table. In deference to their sensibilities, APEC has placed its secretariat in Singapore and has agreed to hold alternate annual meetings in a Southeast Asian country.[5] There are also those who argue that ASEAN's involvement in APEC—and its expansion process by incorporating Vietnam first and, later perhaps, Burma, Laos, and Cambodia—mostly reflects a desire to dilute the influence of China and Japan in the region.

On 15 November 1994, the leaders of the 18 member nations gathered at Bogor, Indonesia, for the second annual APEC summit. The core of its declaration (the boldest international economic initiative, a historic first achieved by co-operation rather than regulation) was fourfold:

- the destruction of all trade barriers to goods manufactured in the region by 2020 in order to construct (rather than an inward-looking trading bloc) a "region" tailor-made for business leaders willing to use it as their operating base;
- the strengthening of an open, multilateral trading system;
- continuing the commitment achieved through the Uruguay Round of GATT/WTO; and
- finalization of the blueprint, drafted at Bogor, to put its declaration into effect during the 1995 meeting in Osaka and 1996 in Manila.

The declaration was approved by a consensus of all 18 nations because, in the words of the Bogor meeting working paper, "Business will go to where bureaucracy is minimal and procedures are straightforward."

In December 1994 in Essen, Germany, the closing document of the EU summit included for the first time a statement on Asia:

"Unless Europe is able to compete in Asia and win, Europe will not be able to compete and win globally."

All of these developments will have an impact not only on which region of the world will attract business, but also on how business will be conducted—in other words, management styles. In an article entitled "Multicultural Perspectives on European and Asian Management", Professor George Hirsch and Frederick Swierczek noted:

> "With the onset of globalisation there is increased interest in the question of whether there is a convergence of management styles and organisational approaches or whether there is a regionalisation taking place. Are particular management styles developing, unique to certain regions of the world, for example Europe or Asia? There is a strong interest in these questions, specifically in Europe because of the changes in the European Community in 1993. Similarly, in Asia, there are significant beginnings of large-scale economic co-operation such as the Asia-Pacific Economic Community (APEC) and the ASEAN Free Trade Area (AFTA). In September APEC which includes Japan, the United States, Australia, China and ASEAN among others established a secretariat in Singapore. AFTA has implemented an open tariff regime to be completed in fifteen years. In the future these efforts will mean greater multicultural management involvement."[6]

## THE FUTURE DEVELOPMENT OF EUROPEAN UNION–ASEAN CO-OPERATION

In the light of all the above considerations and observations, European businesses that are intent on developing their operations in Southeast Asia will inevitably ask: what is the likely future development of co-operation between the European Union and ASEAN? The answer to this question must be seen in the light of the above-mentioned international developments and in the context of changes in national economic and political settings. Many factors come into play in the future development of this relationship, and the literature on the subject is voluminous. However, in terms of European companies looking to Asia for their future expansion, we will consider only a bird's-eye view.

Two observations are relevant with regard to the ASEAN integration process. First, from an economic point of view,

ASEAN has grown rapidly; it has reduced its vulnerability to the international economic environment although it is not yet able to mould it; it has remained dependent on exports to the OECD; and it has been able to continue to integrate by a non-institutionalized process. Second, from a political point of view, ASEAN has been able to focus internally and to build up an effective bond of trust among its member states through avoiding disputes; it has created a foreign policy forum which enables it to speak, and be heard, as one voice; it has persuaded member countries to move towards commercial/industrial integration; and it has secured a preferential trading arrangement which is beginning to increase intra-ASEAN trade.

Economic and political developments in the Southeast Asian region over the last two decades have also transformed aspects of interdependence, as experienced in the region, into a more collective sense of identity. Whether the next two decades will see continued development, and the nature of that development, will depend on both internal and, largely, external factors.

Two observations are relevant, too, with regard to the European Union integration process. First, from an economic point of view, most of the EU nations lag behind the United States and Japan in terms of purchasing power. Only Luxembourg exceeds Japan in this respect, although it still lags behind the United States. Between 1970 and 1990, the US economy created 39 million jobs, compared with just 10 million new jobs in Europe. Over the same period, Europe has continued to widen the social safety net without taking into account fundamental changes in the world economy. European industry has become increasingly less competitive in the market-place, while wages, social security contributions, and unemployment have increased. Economic recovery alone is unlikely to solve the jobs crisis, since an average growth rate of 2.5 per cent is needed just to stand still in a labour market that is expanding by about 0.5 per cent per year. Since the reunification of Germany, Eastern European countries have emerged as rivals to Southeast Asian countries within the European markets, and Western European countries have become even more Eurocentric. If government and business are unable to tackle the problem soon, they will face the spectre of mounting social unrest. The economies of Western Europe have gradually become symbiotic because of the speed and effectiveness of decision-making by individual European companies and not because of any action by governments or the European Union. Despite the fact that there is no unified European currency, this trend is likely to continue. Several plans to increase European competitiveness have been produced by the European Union, the latest by President Jacques Santer's Competitiveness Advisory Group in 1995. However, the future of integration in the European Union rests not on a plan, but on a collective will. This leads to the question: does Europe have the time and/or political will to transform its social and political habits developed over the last 20 years in order to enable the European private sector to compete globally?

From a political point of view, on the other hand, the politics of Europe include opposing interests, fits of national bad temper, and even personal prejudices. The European Union is its own worst public relations enemy, for it makes little effort to explain itself to those it purports to serve.[7] The elaboration of European policies (on trade, fishing rights, or agriculture) is connected with the problems of individual governments, political pressures, and social developments. European integration, as many analysts have observed, was the necessary springboard for Europe to involve itself in foreign policy. However, the Yugoslav crisis and ethnic cleansing indicate that the foreign policies of the member states are still (and many EU business observers forecast that they will remain) dictated by national considerations and that there is little willingness to make sacrifices for the sake of common foreign or security policies.

The economic fallout of German reunification includes destruction of the European Monetary System. Franco-German relations have been strained by Germany touting its newfound political strength, and the country's status as the largest contributor to the EU budget (ECU 85.5 billion in 1994) has angered the German people.

> "It puts in about 28% of the money the union raises each year, yet receives little more than 12% of what the union spends. Britain, without

its rebate, might have to put in as much as 17% of the budget; in fact it puts in 12% and gets around 7% of the EU's spending.'"[8]

The idea of integration was accepted by European governments for very specific political reasons that had more to do with security than standards of living. Some analysts cite the disappearance of the Soviet threat as the reason for European countries' acting as they please, often irresponsibly, and for the waning power of the United States to influence its allies. The removal of such pressures has made political union less imperative. The domestic political pressures behind protectionist and discriminatory trade policies are becoming more difficult to contain. Furthermore, the diseconomies of scale in political and bureaucratic management are already in evidence in the European Union and have given rise to demands for increased participation of EU citizens in decentralized decision-making.

## THE RATIONALE FOR A CO-OPERATIVE FRAMEWORK: SOME CONCLUSIONS

There is mounting pressure to foster regional co-operation arrangements, both institutionalized (as in the European Union) and non-institutionalized (as in ASEAN). This pressure derives from the interdependent nature of the world's economies, from the need to harmonize the characteristics of an increasingly multi-polar world, and from the dependence of Asian economies on an open world trading system and access to the markets of the developed economies.

The attitudes and potential roles of India and China are of significant interest. In fact, although India is beginning to develop a very close relationship with the EU, China's booming economic development and issues of security give it special prominence in the region. The potential for conflict in the South China Sea poses the greatest threat to ASEAN. China, Vietnam, and Taiwan have switched their focus from land-based threats and domestic insurgencies to maritime security concerns. The deep mistrust of China in the region dates back 2000 years, and recent developments have done little to reverse this attitude. The entrepreneurial zeal of mainland Chinese and the interlocking financial networks of the overseas Chinese populations in other Southeast Asian economies are regarded with suspicion, although Malaysia's recent dealings with China may have softened this attitude somewhat.

The flow of US investments into Vietnam following the 1995 lifting of the US embargo is matched in significance by Vietnam's increasing bilateral relations with individual ASEAN nations which led to its joining the Association in 1995.

Economic relations between Taiwan and the ASEAN member nations are being hampered by Taiwan's political concerns, which slow down negotiations by requiring bargaining and decision-making at the highest administrative level (for instance, over the issue of importing annual contract labour from Thailand, the Philippines, and Malaysia) or stall negotiations altogether, as when Taiwan insisted on being called the Republic of China in contracts with Malaysia. Many analysts agree that the conflict and tensions between Taiwan and China loom large in the background and cast a long shadow over Southeast Asia.

Although Taiwan's population is less than a 50th of China, it has the world's second largest foreign-exchange reserves, it is the world's 12th biggest trader, it does almost as much trade with the USA as China.

However, the "healthy ambiguity of one country with two political entities" (as Dr Jason Hy, spokesman for the Taiwanese government, stated in 1993) "continues. On the one hand the Beijing regime has threatened to invade Taiwan if it declares independence. On the other hand, Taiwan is in practice doing its best to preserve its *de facto* independence."

China's March 1996 war games, only 11 miles from some of Taiwan's outlying islands in the Strait, are the latest examples of this continuous, and at times mounting, tension. The meaning of such games, at this time, is four fold: to make a deliberate attempt to damage Taiwan's thriving economy; because the games result in a kind of blockade of the strait; a blatant effort to interfere in Taiwan's first democratic presidential election; a demonstration that Taiwan is a renegade province whose recapture by force China may justify; to draw attention to the contrasts between China's domestic repressions and Taiwan's freedoms. The fact that the USA reacted to the war games by sending war ships and patriot missiles could, in some analysts' view, bring strategic clarity to the long-held American doctrine of "strategic ambiguity" about Taiwan.

America's commitment to Asia is clear. Between 1945 and 1990, and excluding the staggering expenses of the Vietnam War, the United States contributed some US$71 billion in development aid, loans, technical assistance, and other means of economic support to the Asian nations on the western Pacific Rim, and it now takes around 25 per cent of their exports. The United States also provides advanced education to over 150 000 overseas Asian students. (See Chapter 8 for further discussion.) Along with Japan, the United States dominates the Asian stage. At stake in this leadership game are market share, economic well-being, and Japanese-style capitalism versus American-style capitalism. At the close of the 20th century, the Pacific community is well and truly in the foreground of the international scene. The Atlantic community was transformed by the fall of communism in 1989, and the culture that developed around the fight against communism has since been eroded. The poles have shifted, as must Europe's relations with the Pacific community despite the uncertainties inherent in a region without a common military policy, common treaty, or common diplomacy, and with a reliance on conventional means of defence. Those who see only the risks will fail to see the opportunities, as the next chapter discusses.

The lessons to be drawn from world experiences—that is bringing the globalization process to Asia via the European industry—are illustrated in Appendix no. 2.

## ENDNOTES

[1]*International Herald Tribune*, 5 March 1996, p. 6.
[2]*The Economist*, 2 March 1996, p. 34.

[3]From *Far Eastern Economic Review*, 23 June 1994, p. 5. Reproduced by permission.
[4]Sir Leon Brittain, *The Europe We Need*, Hamish Hamilton, London, 1994, p. 15.
[5]*The Economist*, 13 November 1993, p. 81.
[6]From *European Management Journal*, EAP 20th Anniversary Issue 1993, p. 17. Reproduced by permission.
[7]Sir Leon Brittain, *The Europe We Need*, Hamish Hamilton, London, 1994, p. 29.
[8]*The Economist*, 29 January 1994, p. 45.

# 3

# Investing in Southeast Asia: ''Risk'' or ''Opportunity''?

## A MATTER OF PERCEPTION

European businesses tend to see only the risks inherent in operating in the emerging markets of Southeast Asia. Business leaders in Asia, on the other hand, perceive those risks as opportunities. This is not to say that they are inveterate gamblers, but rather that they have a long-term global view based on an innate understanding of and respect for the risk–reward relationship. Astute investors perceive that risk and opportunity are inseparable — in business as in life: one cannot exist without the other. Whether one sees the risk — or the opportunity — first will dictate one's decision-making style and subsequent actions. It is a matter of perception, based on our experiences and beliefs. European business leaders contemplating doing business in Southeast Asian markets will consider the risks and opportunities in light of their own perceptions of the needs of those markets, and the preferred location, timetable, and penetration strategy. Thus, the first act in creating a business bridge between the EU member states and the emerging markets of Southeast Asia must be to change the perception of ''risk'' to one of ''opportunity''.

In this chapter, we consider this matter of perception from five different perspectives — that of the armchair investor, the Asian joint venture partner/consultant, the European business executive, the European Union, and the international expert—before drawing a number of conclusions.

## THE ARMCHAIR INVESTOR'S PERSPECTIVE

Investors the world over are debating the wisdom of taking a punt on Southeast Asia's latest "economic miracle". On 3 April 1995, *Barron's* magazine published a debate on the question of whether recent strength portends a resumption of brisk growth or whether it is merely a brief respite before another onslaught of selling. The participants were divided in their feelings. Some felt that they were not prepared to pay the price for setting up a company in Asia—the risks were enormous. Others felt that only by moving to the country could they understand the local culture, economics and politics. The risks for them were small when the returns could be so much more positive.

Two contrasting attitudes. Some emphasized the opportunity of making money by accepting the risk of moving from the Western financial capitals to the Asian ones. For others, it was clearly the risk of moving of utmost priority, not the opportunity of making money. That is, to take the risk to abandon one's own culture, i.e. certainty for uncertainty, to work on a business opportunity in Asia was surely not, for him, a workable proposition. For the former the opportunity made him move. For the latter the risk made him stay.

## THE ASIAN JOINT VENTURE PARTNER/ CONSULTANT'S PERSPECTIVE

Surveys on how Asian entrepreneurs view the performance of foreign companies engaged in joint ventures in their countries reveal many weaknesses in the consultancy industry in Southeast Asia. Foreign firms are criticized for ignoring local views, knowledge, and expertise, and imposing knowledge on Asians rather than sharing it. Local cultural values and customs tend to be ignored, and there is usually little familiarity with the local Asian language. A short-term view of business co-operation tends to predominate over a long-term view, so that joint ventures are largely based on an association of convenience, where the main role of the local firm is to satisfy government requirements, instead of a genuine partnership. Other reasons given by Asian entrepreneurs for the failure of joint ventures include a lack of rapport between the partners; a lack of opportunities for local partners to exercise decision-making authority; inadequate supervision of young and inexperienced personnel engaged in important tasks; clashes over issues such as the use of expatriate women as project managers in, say, the construction industry; interruption of the flow of funds as a result of mismanagement on the part of the employing agency; a lack of firm policy guidelines or frequent policy changes; the inability of the employing agency to make, and stand by, decisions; and excessive intervention by employing agency officials.

The term "joint venture" itself, in the context of a developing country, implies a superior–inferior relationship, and the concept of "technology transfer and training" exacerbates this tension. The cultural gap created by differences in language, time concepts, priorities, and procedures causes friction, along with the assumption that the transfer operates only in one direction. Transfer is less problematic in the hard sciences and engineering, where there is less dependence on bridging the cultural gap, than in management and the social sciences.

The time span of joint ventures is also important. In the short term, transfer is minimal, with *ad hoc*, infrequent associations. Maximum transfer can only be achieved through a long-term (essentially permanent) relationship, but this is often made difficult by issues of time, money, and manpower.

Local joint venture partners are aware that government insistence upon joint ventures can create a poor atmosphere and may lead to pro forma agreements and merely political contacts. Nevertheless, despite the difficulties facing joint ventures, they are often successful. Conditions identified by local partners as favouring successful transfer include an awareness of the opportunities and a strong motivation to proceed; culturally sensitive expatriate personnel who provide every opportunity for local partners to use local know-how in solving problems; an emphasis, by local firms, on planning their own long-term future; adequate capital to take advantage of new skills and knowledge; a continuous and long-term relationship between the venture partners; an emphasis on transfer of engineering and hardware; an adequate educational base among local professionals; government encouragement and recognition of success; and considerate, constructive, generous, and optimistic decision-makers in both partner firms.

The presence of these factors is no guarantee of a successful venture, however, as the selection of the foreign consultant may itself be unsatisfactory, as in the case of World Bank and Asian Development Bank-financed projects. Currently, the "proposal method" is used, whereby a large number of consultancy firms are identified, from among which a shortlist of as many as 15 firms is compiled. These firms are then invited to submit proposals to the employing agency. Each shortlisted firm is supplied with the terms of reference, on the basis of which they prepare a technical proposal and a financial proposal. The firms are usually led to believe that the financial proposal will only be examined if the technical proposal meets the approval of the employing agency. The successful firm is then invited to negotiate its fees.

The weakness of the system, apart from the tremendous waste of time and other resources by the unsuccessful firms, is that successful firms build upon their previous successes by wording their proposals in such a way as to meet the requirements of the selection committee, and thus make it very difficult for new Asian firms to break in. The objective of the exercise is to have one's proposal accepted; implementation is a different issue. The net result is that projects continue to be awarded to the same few firms whose positions are all but entrenched. As a result no new blood is introduced onto the scene, and Asian consultancies are bearing the brunt of this.

Asian consulting firms have had many opportunities to witness at first hand the results of consultancy services employing prestigious firms based in London or New York, or other equally remote centres. Vast sums are spent on engaging their services and generating lavishly produced reports for submission to the development agencies. Many such proposals are rejected as being impossible to implement. Survey information may have been unavailable, or where data was available it may be unreliable. Some proposals are simply over-ambitious, and many fail to take account of local conditions. Nevertheless, many projects do go into development, usually on the basis of *ad hoc* plans drawn up by people on the spot who have had to draw on their knowledge and resourcefulness to tackle situations as they arose. In the field of human settlement planning, for example, the cultural element and the fact that one is dealing with human communities, requires the consultant to have an in-depth exposure to the issue in order to be able to understand the root causes and ramifications of problems and to suggest appropriate and effective solutions.

In the Asian consultant's view, the main issue is self-reliance. There are justifications other than romantic nationalism in the quest for self-reliance in consultancy services. One such justification is the role of local values, cultures, and national perspectives in managing projects. The commitment of human and other resources to projects, which in some cases is irreversible, is a politically significant assertion of national sovereignty. For this reason, local professionals must bear the greater responsibility for decision-making. Their familiarity with the local value context is a decided advantage, especially in situations where the best choice is a compromise among many non-technical factors.

The recommendations of local professionals who are attuned to the sensibilities of their countrymen are likely to be more credible and acceptable than those of foreign consultants. The mere fact that local consultants will be more familiar with the idiosyncracies of local bureaucrats improves the chances of projects being accepted and implemented.

The biggest component in consultancy contracts is professional services. In this area, substantial savings could be realized by engaging local consultants. Self-reliance saves dollars, an issue of some concern in countries plagued by foreign currency difficulties.

There is a place for foreign consultancies in Asia, although their effectiveness will be enhanced if they have a stake in a country's self-reliance through the use of local affiliates. Given time and opportunity, foreign consultants can acquire a "national perspective" and their instincts in regard to non-technical factors might even be sharper than the locals'. However, nationalistic sentiments are very real in developing countries and the presence of foreign consultants provokes resentment. One of the best ways of dealing with this is to encourage increasing local participation in projects. When foreign consultants and local experts consider each other as peers, resentment can be overcome by a sense of fraternity among professionals. However, this will only be possible with increased self-confidence of local consultants. And self-confidence derives from further training.

The training component in a consultancy contract must be paid for, and effective training is expensive. The host country must be willing to pay the cost, and the lending institutions to give support. Expertise is the prime corporate asset of consultancy firms and it is unrealistic to expect them to share know-how and experience out of sheer altruism. Training should be part of the legitimate output of a project, and not just a superficial rider to the contract.

The Asian consultant is eager to learn and adopt the end result of the process, adapt it and grow. He takes the possibility of working on a project funded by an international financing institution as a welcome opportunity to participate in the development of his country, perhaps even without making a profit. To maximize it, he had to take the risk to joint venture with a foreign company. And he took it. In making his decision to act, the maximization of the opportunity was the driving force.

## THE EUROPEAN BUSINESS EXECUTIVE'S PERSPECTIVE

European businesses already operating in the emerging markets of Southeast Asia have weighed the opportunities against the risks and have developed a vision of what Europe's role in the region could be. They are laying the necessary foundations to turn that vision into a reality. They have found an answer to the question of *why* they should invest in Southeast Asia and are proceeding with the *how*. Consider the following typical comment: "The big firms look after themselves. To ask a small company to take on Asia alone is a bit much, but within a consortium it is possible. In the same way we have to keep smaller firms informed about opportunities in large projects, and not treat them as one-off opportunities. But there is no follow-up."

The matter of how to invest is of critical concern to those European companies searching for a point of entry into the Asian markets. But most of these efforts are incapable of efficiently taking on the international competition in Asia in general, and Southeast Asia in particular. What if they were to strike up alliances in Europe — through joint ventures, for example? Could they prepare themselves more effectively in Europe by planning strategic approaches to the Asian markets? Could institutions like the European Investment Bank play a partnership role? In seeking answers to these questions, it is necessary to consider the competitive pressures, the needs of the client country, and the formation of Europe Inc. along Japanese and American lines. We will consider each of these in turn.

A European manufacturing group present in Asia since the 1970s has an Asian market strategy spanning an array of activities including: formation of joint ventures with local partners in Malaysia, Indonesia, Thailand, India and China; producing its products at those local plants; sponsoring football teams, because in many parts of Asia football games are widely followed on pay TV; joint ventures with local manufacturing companies in rallies. One of its Asian corporate executives, visiting Europe from his Asian base, considering the role of European companies in Asian markets made the following reflections.

The success of Europe's competitors, especially Japan and the United States, in winning major business in developing countries, and particularly in Southeast Asia, is a source of admiration and envy. There is also some suspicion that these economic superpowers say one thing in international fora but act quite differently in practice. What else could account for their being so much more successful than their European competitors?

The two principal development areas in the world of prime interest to Western business are Southeast Asia and Central Europe. Southeast Asia, the more politically stable of the two, has a faster growth rate, a larger population, and a more successful work ethic (in terms of diligence, skills, and entrepreneurship). Furthermore, its natural resources are as abundant as those in Central Europe. Consequently, it is attracting the greater share of attention.

The United States now has a greater trade flow with the countries of the Pacific Rim than with Europe. Japan is the world's second-largest economy, although it has been predicted by some commentators that China will outrank both Japan and the United States within 20 years.

Central Europe is presently in political and economic turmoil and suffers from a central bureaucracy with its attendant inefficiencies and corruption. The situation is no different from that in some Asian countries 20 years ago and in areas of Africa today. This suggests that it may take some years for the political revolution in Central Europe to be transformed into an economic revolution. In the interim, the business and financial risks are greater than many Western businesses will wish to face, particularly as there are more attractive prospects elsewhere.

However, Western European businesses must realize that the United States and, especially, Japan regard the Pacific Rim as their backyard, and thus it will be difficult to displace them there. Competition in Western Europe's own backyard, Central Europe, looks likely to be less fierce, at least in the short term, although there are some businessmen who would argue: "If you allow your opponent to be comfortable in his backyard while he is attacking you in yours, that's a silly strategy."

Therefore, while Southeast Asia will undoubtedly provide the most attractive prospects for the next decade and beyond, European businesses will need to compete with their counterparts in the United States, Japan, and other Asian "Tigers" (Japan, Taiwan, Singapore, and Hong Kong), all of whom are well established. In contrast, Central Europe is more open to Western European business and the opportunities there should be exploited before others do so. (The multinational population of the United States, many of whom have ethnic ties to Europe, makes it a particularly strong competitor in this arena.)

Apart from the demands of global competition, European businesses must consider the needs of the countries in which they seek to invest. Just as it is every supplier's aim to extract the highest price for its products in the market-place, so it is every buyer's objective to obtain those products at the lowest price. The buyer's philosophy also applies to the client countries who strive to obtain the best commercial/financial deal for their country. The United States and Japan, with their market-led focus, have long had a clear understanding of the needs of their clients and offer attractive financial packages which have sometimes transformed otherwise non-competitive commercial tenders into winning bids.

Japan well understands its customers' tender criteria and consequently offers a low initial bid price with equally low interest rate yen loans. The profit is reaped subsequently with very high priced servicing and spare parts. Many customers in the emerging Asian markets have found the overall price paid to the Japanese supplier to be higher than for European goods, particularly if the appreciation of the yen is taken into account. However, most customers have relatively simple tendering processes which cannot account for such indeterminate fluctuations. The Japanese in particular seem more able (with their protected home prices) than Europeans to exploit these tender limitations. The Japanese are also the major "aid for trade" providers and are recognized as such by the client countries. They possess another superior advantage in being able to offer a complete package through a front trading company and by controlling internal competition.

The United States has skilfully used various trade instruments to their advantage. How often has Europe witnessed a restriction lifted only when the United States is ready to announce a major trade deal? While the United States sings the praises of free trade, it surreptitiously finances, at concession rates, exports which it considers of strategic importance. It is little wonder that the client countries are acutely aware of the influence of the United States in world trade.

In Europe, the French perhaps have been most adept at putting together attractively financed packages, and in many ways they provide a model of government/industry partnership. Latterly the Italians have also demonstrated a certain flair in ignoring conventions when business ventures have a high strategic value. The British, after a period of vacillation, are starting to respond with aid funding of strategic sectors and key markets, but they are hampered by their desire for fair play and observation of agreed conventions. The Germans are still too preoccupied with unification and their eastern neighbours to play much of a role in the wider world. Economic conditions in Europe in the immediate future are likely to leave their mark on the available finance for aid funding of overseas projects. Japan and, to a lesser extent, the United States may suffer similar pressures, although it is unlikely that Japan would willingly relinquish its overseas markets.

If Europe is to emulate its successful competitors, then the model to follow is Japan, which approaches all foreign business according to the principle of Japan Inc. Very rarely is there genuine internal competition (although there is often artificial competition in order to comply with regulations), and a total turnkey package is usually marshalled through a single trading company. There is rarely a problem in offering the most competitive finance, and there is a close partnership between government and industry.

As a leading economy, Europe fails to use its combined strength in the world markets. Any multinational co-operation that exists derives from business linkages (for example, ABB, GEC/Alcatel and Siemens) despite government rivalries. Such companies can co-operate in order to defeat external competitors for foreign business, but they rarely defeat American competitors because there is no central funding agency which could be the catalyst to bring European companies together.

European governments cannot expect business to operate for the greater good of Europe. Business will always operate for its own benefit. Japanese and American businesses operate on behalf of their countries only because their governments work in close partnership with them and provide central funding to support the export effort. If Europe wants to use its collective muscle, then it is the role of Europe's governments to provide the co-ordination and incentives to do so. There are certainly companies in Europe capable of providing project leadership equal to the Japanese and the Americans. What is less evident is the leadership from government in providing equal funding support.

One world-leading group based in Europe saw in the Asia/Southeast Asian markets a unique opportunity not to be missed. In maximizing the opportunity it evaluated and accepted the risks rooted in producing value-added products in Southeast Asian markets. Assessing them and taking them, it was able to joint venture with Asian partners. On the basis of this performance, looking back at Europe, from Asia, and its company's performance it identified some of the typical problems which make some European companies see and perceive the risk before the opportunity.

## THE EUROPEAN UNION'S PERSPECTIVE

In January 1995 at the World Economic Forum at Davos, Switzerland, the EU Commission President, Jacques Santer called his audience's attention to the fact that the EU was simply not pulling its weight on the international stage in the foreign and security policy areas because of its uncoordinated intergovernmentalism which is still too frequently the *modus vivendi*.

The following month, speaking before the EU Parliament, President Santer presented the 1995 Work Programme, including statements on the economy, regional policy, R&D, information, energy and development, transport, the international scene, and other fields. His comments on the international scene echoed his conclusion at Davos where he suggested that we Europeans are not only failing to co-ordinate our policies adequately, but also failing in our strategic planning.

This institutionalized view emphasizes the risks of lack of co-ordinated policies among the 15 EU members. They are seen first, well before the opportunity, because they are perceived to be the obstacles in the way of developing the role of Europe in Southeast Asia—then materialized in the very first Asem summit. Taking the opportunity to make this summit a success, the EU presented a package of measures to emphasize Europe's quest for a new role in Asia. In so doing, it took the risk of having to show the colours of its true new will towards Asia by deciding to liberalize its markets to Asia accepting, thus, Asian demands. A move which could equal the results of APEC's Osaka 1995, which will start being implemented at the November 1996 meeting in Manila. The opportunities and risks involved in the implementation of the APEC agreement are—as previously mentioned—of tremendous importance to private businesses. So too are the risks and the opportunities involved in Asia.

## THE INTERNATIONAL EXPERT'S PERSPECTIVE

At the 1995 meeting of the World Economic Forum (WEF) there was an overwhelming consensus about what European companies have to do to increase their competitiveness.

- Identify priority growth markets (high-growth emerging economies such as Malaysia and India, giant economies such as China and India, and so on).
- Consider their attractiveness in terms of cost. Trim high social and labour costs. (Labour costs in developing countries are roughly US$2 an hour, compared with around US$20 an hour in developed countries.)
- Deregulate unions.
- Develop a structure of strategically conceived alliances. A business should be seen as a global network of relationships for sourcing.

- Establish local, insider positions to allow leverage of imported technical skills.
- Put more money into education and training.
- Build something that is self-sustaining.
- Do not choose a manufacturing site on the basis of labour costs alone; find a way to add value or development. It is no longer sufficient to ship in finished goods or even just to manufacture in a given country. Transfer some R&D know-how in the form of experienced people who will be able to integrate into the local culture.

Within the cosy and exclusive alpine resort of Davos, Switzerland where 2000 businessmen, academics and politicians gather every year to attend the World Economic Forum (WEF), it is much easier to consider risks and opportunities. The sole purpose of such gatherings is to exchange ideas, not master a common will to spring into action and to maximize a given opportunity. Yet, those who do not participate, get the impression that something important has been decided there, i.e. a risk has been considered and accepted to maximize a unique opportunity. Indeed, the preaching of the gospel of free trade, being a fashionable subject, seems an activity everybody loves to share. But no decision of any kind is actually taken. It means that the only risks and opportunities to be taken in such a forum are to be in the right room—there are several sessions being held at the same time—to attend the preferred conference, discovering what is in the speakers'/participants' minds and, if possible, meet the right people and exchange cards with them. Therefore, the Forum's halls yearly echo the European businessmen's concerns about the lack of a common political will to attack the competitive problem of European industry in Southeast Asia.

## CONCLUSION

What these five different ways of seeing and perceiving risk and opportunity show is the clash between two cultures: preservation and innovation. The first is protectionism, a culture living in the past. It is cherished by many followers and offered to them by the few, their "leaders". It is the protection from anything that is uncertain, from the terror of changing by innovating, from the risk innate to any abandonment of the reassuring tradition. It is a culture sponsoring security, in a world which is insecure; a safe job even if not well paid and gratifying, the safe market because dominated by politics, not experiencing the cold winds—potentially invigorating—of the international competition. It is a culture to privilege the minimization of risk in the short term not the maximization of the opportunity in the long term; searching for and finding mass consensus, continuity, promising protection not economic, legal, cultural and moral incentives to the construction of the new.

The culture of resistance to change will allow only the very first steps to be taken on the long march to improved European competitiveness. It should be aiming at maximizing the business opportunities offered by the Southeast Asian markets. The export opportunities offered the engine of growth and recovery for Europe. It ran at full speed in 1994–5 allowing Germany to increase its global exports by 7.9 per cent; the UK by 15 per cent; Spain by 17 per cent; Italy by 9.6 per cent. This dramatic growth was made possible by a variety of factors working at the same time: currency devaluation; the 1994 world surge in growth; the surge of investments by foreign companies (i.e. non European) wishing to enter the European market; the efforts by medium and small-sized companies facing the hard fact: export or die; for some of them exports were a parachute, a bolt-on activity to be pulled only in an emergency.

This culture of resistance against drastic changes and adapt them to the actual needs of the situation at hand, brought a revival of the European economy and of these companies' fortunes and competitiveness. It was, though, a competitiveness not brought by increased know-how, better training, better plants and greater efficiency and productivity, but by maximizing short-term opportunities, and the earnings that came with them, through pricing and very little investment. This slow-down in investment, as well as rising inflation and rising interest rates, the ease with which the companies increased their profits and the need, in these situations to control/reduce costs represented the real risk that these companies did not tackle. Instead, shrouded in the preservation culture, these companies went to Southeast Asian markets to have a quick bite at their business opportunities and make a good profit to run back to Europe.

The second culture is one of opportunity. It lives in the tomorrow. It makes one find one's own bearings on the road of uncertainty, to reach unusual objectives associated with creative exploration. It is a culture imposing the logic of innovation, breaking through the protectionist dams. It is a culture accepting the fact that investors and innovators have to alter their once settled ways. Thus, on the one hand innovators must place far greater emphasis on gaining intimate knowledge of the product to be researched and developed, to target appropriately the needs of the Southeast Asian market, and its projected growth rates; co-investing in the opportunity with well chosen partners; building and supplementing the management team with technology management experts whenever required. On the other hand, investors have to reconcile themselves with a simple business reality: the revenues their innovative products can generate depend on the quality of the planning activities, which have to be strategic; joint venture ideas, which have to be accurately assessed and alternatively evaluated, with sound partners (to be properly selected, especially across a variety of criteria including also cross-cultural communication lines); reviewing performances (critically and periodically) to identify what can be done better next time around and the quality of the sales promotion campaign (thus marketing has to be aggressive).

In so doing European innovators and investors seeking to enter individual markets in Southeast Asia, operate on the basis of a driving business opportunity vision. It will allow them to operate on the basis of clearly defined and designed strategies, precise allocation of incentives and responsibilities, with built-in flexibility, evaluation and acceptance of the risks involved. Thus, their competitiveness will dramatically increase because of the greater efficiency and productivity achieved, improved knowledge and better training. These companies can maximize their business opportunities in Southeast Asian markets by learning and listening to what the potential needs of the country and its potential clients are. They can then make their significant contribution towards satisfying their clients and by sharing knowledge be involved in their culture and everyday life.

The inward-looking Europe of the past has no place in a global market-place made possible through technological advances, deregulation, and world-wide competition. The onus lies with transnational companies and medium-sized to small firms to counter this "fortress" mentality derived from perceptions of risk, by adopting an outward-looking approach based on the perception of opportunities and confidence in their ability to compete with their American and Japanese counterparts.

European businesses must have a vision of the future, and of the substance and nature of their role in it (see Figure 3.1). The main problem in *developing* such a vision lies in changing the perception of risk to the perception of opportunity. The main problem in *implementing* that vision lies in the willingness to learn and adapt. This implies successful cross-cultural communication, the subject of Part II of this book.

*Requirements:*

Have an attractive and clear view of the future which:

- can be shared
- is ambitious
- motivates
- should stretch people to achieve more than they might ever have thought possible
- is articulated and effectively communicated.

It should not be seen as just words on paper but should

- act as a guide to conduct realistic action
- build understanding on how to put down roots and transform it into reality
- aim at building a long-term relationship with customers
- count on effective delegation
- count on managers being equipped to effectively handle the new demands of the vision thrust upon them, by involving their employees, their security and their own commitment to the achievement of agreed objectives.

*Source*: Corrado G. M. Letta, *Managing Destructive Processes Creatively* (1993 unpublished)

**Figure 3.1** *The vision.*

# Part II
## MANAGING CROSS-CULTURAL COMMUNICATION

# 4
# A Comparison of European and Asian Corporate Cultures

## INTRODUCTION

A productive partnership between the European Union member states and the countries of Southeast Asia would create a two-way flow of exports, know-how in all its forms, the ability to build up organizational and market-oriented linkages, and money flows. Exporting and investing are the primary means for Europe to participate in the emerging markets of Southeast Asia, which account for 45 per cent of world-wide market growth. Europe's participation is important in terms of ensuring its own technological progress, economies of scale, and, ultimately, the creation of wealth and jobs in Europe.

The most critical factor in the success of an international joint venture is the actual performance of the expatriate resident manager in the host country, as perceived not by the European headquarters but by the local Asian partners. Managers' performance is influenced by their depth of understanding of their own culture and that of the host country; by their ability to conduct cross-cultural dialogues; by their skill in negotiating, clinching, and implementing the joint venture; by their role as resident manager; and by how effectively the delegation of authority from European headquarters to the Southeast Asian subsidiaries has been clearly designed and implemented and how they effectively delegate decision-making authority to local managers.

The challenges facing expatriate resident managers raise issues of resistance to change, conflict resolution, group dynamics, diffusion of products and ideas, communicative influences, the process of innovation, and the problems of learning and relearning. Relearning requires unlearning old ways in order to be able to fully adapt to the new local culture. The process might be compared to a river that meanders across the plains, depositing the sand and mud picked up in earlier environments, and extending its delta into the shallow waters bordering the new environment.

Europe first became aware of Southeast Asia when Marco Polo returned from China at the end of the 13th century and told of campaigns waged by the Chinese against barbarian kingdoms to the south. Thereafter, Europeans thought of the region as a distant and mysterious treasure house. Today, with no effective private business lobby in Europe—apart from the European Round Table of Industrialists—able to influence the shaping of European policy towards Asia and to forge Europe Inc. in the region, this sense of distance and mystery remains a significant factor in the lack of an assertive involvement of medium-sized to small European businesses in Southeast Asia.

This chapter considers how the learning/relearning process could be used in reversing European ignorance of the cultures of Southeast Asia and thus opening the way to effective cross-cultural communication and productive business partnerships.

## WHAT IS CULTURE?

There are perhaps as many definitions of culture as there are people. One's experience of culture depends on one's role in it. Sociologists might define it as "the ultimate system of social control where people act appropriately and monitor their own standards and behaviour." An international marketeer, who needs to know which factors influence customers' needs and wants, may define culture as "the learned ways of group living and group responses to various stimuli". Rather than try to define culture, we will focus on its content. Culture consists of the values, attitudes, beliefs, and customs of a society. Paramount among these are religious beliefs, ethnic and nationalistic symbols and traditions, as well as secular views on the human condition and human relations, individual and social priorities, morality, and rights and obligations, all of which may be institutionalized to varying degrees. Culture also includes the social activities that express and enrich (while also transforming) those values, attitudes, beliefs, and customs. Activities range from grass-roots forms (such as the production of folk art and handicrafts, the creation and performance of folk music and dance, and popular festivities and other collective entertainment) to specialized cultural forms (literature, music, painting, theatre, dance, films, television, and so on). The products they generate become, in turn, part of the society's culture.

An outline of the global communication process and cross-cultural communication issues and problems is presented in Appendix no. 3.

## CORPORATE CULTURE

One type of culture that has attracted a lot of interest in the last two decades is management, or corporate, culture. Corporate culture is a perfect example of a modern interdisciplinary field of research borrowing concepts, perspectives, models, and methods from a wide variety of disciplines, from ethnography to accounting. In this book, our main interest is in the different management orientations of expatriate and local managers operating in joint ventures in developing countries, and how in today's transcultural world and global economy it is necessary to be able to co-exist with other cultures on many different levels.

One way of achieving this is through comprehensive, tailor-made training programmes for business people working in or planning on penetrating specific Southeast Asian markets.

Training programmes imply the development of new knowledge as a result of exposure to unfamiliar environmental stimuli, followed by its application in the business environment. Ultimately it implies change, which is essential if one is to stay ahead in the competition game.

It is not possible to lump all of the cultures of the region together and operate according to a single strategy. A tailor-made strategy is essential for penetrating local markets, and becoming adapted to and integrated into those markets. In a transcultural world, managers must be taught how to do business overseas on a day-to-day basis: how to communicate, negotiate, delegate, anticipate and resolve conflicts in the context of a culture that differs in most respects from their own.

The most important aspects of doing business in Southeast Asian countries are often masked by myths about Asia which, rather than contribute to a deeper understanding, mystify it. Managers who jet in and out of the region, instead of living and working there, will have very little chance of decoding the messages encoded in the local culture. The commitment to a venture must be multi-layered, involving company headquarters, individual expatriate managers, national governments, and the European Union as a whole. Without such a commitment, Europe will miss out on the opportunity to respond to the expressed need in Southeast Asia for a strong European business presence and so lose a strategic advantage over its competitors.

Given the current state of evolution of the European Union, a commitment to Asia seems to have been well timed with the March 1996 Asem summit. European companies are reorganizing and restructuring in order to become more competitive on the world business scene and within the single European market. This restructuring is not only confined to major companies such as Pirelli, Volkswagen, Philips and ICI, but is also spreading to small and medium-sized companies. Although the transnational companies have greater experience in penetrating foreign markets than do small and medium-sized businesses, which make up the majority of European companies, both have a huge untapped potential in this area.

## The Need for a Unified "European" Business Culture

European businesses need to co-operate in presenting a coherent and unified business image in Asia. An example of the current piece-meal, divisive approach can be found in the members of the European Construction Industry (ECI), who have failed, despite their technological know-how, to win their rightful share of the estimated US$3 trillion of infrastructure development in Asia because of the lack of both a unified approach to marketing and a learning culture. This is discussed in further detail in Chapter 7.

Colin Randlesome's *Business Cultures in Europe* is an excellent portrayal of the Spanish, German, French, Italian, and UK business cultures. As Randlesome explains, the book "leads to a better appreciation of the structures and strategies of industries, markets and consumers' preferences in the countries covered."[1] But this individualistic approach is not what Malaysians, Indonesians, and Thais expect when searching for ways to do business with Europe. They perceive Europe as one nation state on the global stage and expect *Europeans* to have a strong presence in their markets. Some might argue that there will never be a single European mentality, that the traditional ideological rivalry between the nations is too entrenched. However, if the supranational institutions working on strategic plans for Europe in the next century sponsored the training of young managers from different EU member states to enable them to become effective *European*-minded executives concerned with *Europe*'s interests on the global stage, a vital step would be taken in forging Europe Inc.

Southeast Asia requires skilled performance by expatriate European managers with a long-term commitment to their host country and business partners. Skilled performance is dependent upon effective cross-cultural communication. The role of cross-cultural analysis is necessarily important because of the way people are conditioned by the culture of the country in which they live. A systematic comparison of the similarities and differences in the material and behavioural aspects of the nations comprising the European Union and Southeast Asia will provide an understanding of Southeast Asian markets and market segments and enable strategies to be developed for penetrating the most appropriate markets.

Cross-cultural analysis will not eliminate the differences between Europe and Southeast Asia, but it may help to minimize European cultural bias in interpreting and understanding the countries in the region and would provide a huge advantage over Europe's competitors. The managers of European companies investing, or planning to invest, in Asia must be especially sensitive to the influence of their own national cultures on their interpretation of events, behaviour, and information while living and working overseas.

## A COMPARISON OF EUROPEAN AND ASIAN CORPORATE CULTURES

Corporate cultures reflect the underlying values of the culture as a whole. Culture is to the organization what personality is to the individual—a hidden yet unifying theme that mobilizes it and gives it direction. It influences how what is happening both within and outside the company will be perceived and the way in which managers respond. A corporate culture that incorporates learning and fosters the ability to change will produce a healthy organization and healthy cross-cultural relationships. In India, for example, the country manager of Kellogg had to rethink the company's marketing of its Wheat Flakes and Corn Flakes breakfast cereals because people were eating them straight from the packet as a crunchy, sweet snack. Consumers' breakfast needs were met by substituting Basmati Flakes, a hot, savoury, soft product more in keeping with the traditional Asian breakfast. The positive result of this cultural clash, with its potential risk of a loss of market share, was increased knowledge of the market which created an opportunity to develop a culturally relevant product and, in the process, increase market share.

In Southeast Asia, employees, suppliers, and customers are treated as members of the family circle. John Tu and David Sun, owners of Kingston Technology (a computer company in Fountain Valley, California), successfully exported this mindset to the United States by instilling in all the people they dealt with such Asian family values as trust, loyalty, and mutual support in an industry where "screwing your customers—let alone suppliers and employees—is second nature. Their philosophy is: If you make your customers, workers and suppliers happy, your business will prosper."[2]

Most European companies' attitudes towards developing markets in Asia have been shaped by a crisis mentality based on the drive to cut costs. Theirs is a "play safe" corporate culture focused on "conquering" the Asian markets and increasing the level of exports rather than forming joint ventures. Thus, their planning has been flawed from the start. The average company, lacking a solid learning culture and so failing to learn from its experiences and turn defeat into victory, becomes reluctant to commit its capital to market development and higher sales. The managers of such companies are so obsessed with the bottom line that they barely have time to be civil to their employees. Inevitably, the survival of companies operating in such a culture of crisis is threatened because their prime resource, their employees, lack motivation and commitment and may harbour resentment against the company if they feel unable to move to a better one. In 1995, Napier Scott, a British recruitment consultant, found in a survey that more than half of the males surveyed, and a third of the women, felt less loyalty to their organizations than 12 months previously. They felt they weren't respected within the organization, and that promises about matters such as job specifications, promotions prospects, and redundancy levels hadn't been kept.

Most European companies have a non-learning culture: experience, expertise, and ideas are jealously guarded because information is thought to be power. The aim is to achieve success of the individual. The President and CEO of Compaq Computer Corporation, Eckhard Pfeiffer, had this to say about learning:

> "Many businesses miss the next play, the next breakpoint, the next shift in the rules of the game. Why? because nothing is harder than casting aside the thinking, strategies and biases that propelled a business to success. The inability to do this, however, may prevent your business from seeing its next opportunity, responding to emerging competitors, and sustaining leadership. We all need to learn how to avoid being trapped by our stalled base—of current customers and competitors, market researchers, and mental models that may overly rely on the quantifiable and the analytic. Companies need to learn to unlearn, to discard yesterday's wisdom and find a fresh viewpoint.'"[3]

In Asia, success is equated with an ability to adapt to the local culture and to participate actively in it. Expatriate managers based in a Southeast Asian country who associate in and out of the office mainly with other expatriates will do themselves and their organization little good in a culture that places as high a value on personal relationships as it does on shared professional know-how.

Other differences in cultural attitudes between Europe and Asia are identified in Table 4.1.

The following three examples show these differences in action.

Europeans attending classical music performances in concert halls throughout Europe have been electrified and puzzled by

***Table 4.1*** *Comparison of cultural values in Europe and Asia*

| Europe | Asia |
|---|---|
| Personal achievement | One's own country's achievement |
| Reluctance to learn | Willingness to learn/respect for learning |
| Rights to work/rights on the job | Hard work and duties on the job |
| Focus on "me" (self-realization) | Focus on "us" (social realization) |
| Safeguarding old ideas | Openness to new ideas |
| Short-term goals | Long-term goals |
| Personal freedom | Self-discipline |
| Subjective | Objective |
| Thinking for oneself | Community self-reliance |
| Complacency | Creativity |
| Vertical structures | Horizontal structures |
| Taking it easy | Hard work |
| Pain denying | Pain accepting |
| Admission of error does not necessarily lead to loss of face | Admission of error leads to loss of face |
| Perception of risk | Perception of opportunity |
| Doom and gloom | Booming confidence |

the violin playing of a number of young Asian musicians. What was once a field dominated by Europeans is being taken over by Asians. How has this come about? Through dedication and commitment of the musicians' families. Asian families are highly motivated and focused on the achievement of high standards. Children are supported, encouraged, and inspired by the whole family, and have no problem working long hours in order to achieve their long-term goals. European children tend to have both parents working in order to provide them with material advantages, but they lack the psychological and spiritual support which gives their Asian peers a competitive edge.

Surveys have shown that the cultural gulf between Europeans and Asians is apparent as early in life as primary school. At the centre of the child's life is the mother. Asian mothers have a central role in continuing their children's education at home through their insistence that the child spend long hours doing homework. They tend to be very critical of their children's achievements, while Europeans are generally less demanding.

Interracial marriages are commonplace today, but attitudes in Europe to marriages between Europeans and Asians reflect a continuing ignorance of Asia. When the Pakistani cricketer Imran Kahn married the daughter of British–French billionnaire Sir James Goldsmith, the public evaluation of the marriage revealed stereotypical attitudes and a complacency about Western superiority. Lahore, where the couple would make their home, was described in the British press as "a stinking hell-hole and dour prison of purdah", when in fact it is a beautiful city at the cultural, intellectual, and political heart of Pakistan.

These examples illustrate that racism and ignorance are alive and well in Europe. The lack of understanding of Asia produces an unwillingness to learn to understand, and many Asians in Europe have become scapegoats and the victims of violence. They are seen as being caught between two cultures (say, between being a Buddhist and a German citizen) and not belonging totally to either. In reality, they—especially the second-generation Asian citizens of Europe—are the new

Europeans. The cultural clash is not present in the person, but within the society which fears and excludes them.

Asians have long been a driving force in European business, with their newsagents, chemists, restaurants, and late-night corner shops. Their success is fuelled by working seven days a week, 15 hours a day, by taking risks and mobilizing the entire family. In Britain, Asian businesses contribute around £8 billion, approximately 2 per cent, of GDP each year. Large numbers of Indian, Pakistani, and Bangladeshi businessmen are appearing at the leading edge of the British business scene, diversifying and expanding across international frontiers, based on the same work ethic. They have ventured into every type of business, from food (the Tilda and Europa groups) to electronics (Binatone), from hotels, steel and plastics (the Capara Group, a £400 million business empire employing 5000 people world-wide) to fashion (Joe Bloggs). Businesses such as these, by combining an Eastern work ethic with Western education, have an international outlook that has enabled them to expand throughout Europe and into Asia. The expansion and diversification of Asia in Europe provides a lesson in transculturalism that, if heeded by European businesses, would enable Europe to successfully compete in Asia and, thus, in the global sphere.

In June 1994, in Singapore, the Asia Society and Dow Jones organized a conference on the topic of Asian values. The main issue discussed was the West's fitness to judge Asia.

> "With the new affluence has come a confidence most clearly reflected in Asia's new dynamic with the West. Leaders here are no longer content to sit back and let Europe and America dictate terms. This creates new frictions, especially in areas such as trade and human rights. Hence the reference to Asian values. When Asia looks to America today, for example, they do not see the solution to these problems [of being infected by Westerners' diseases such as: decay in order, lack of discipline, disappearance of family life, erosion of basic education and ever increasing problems of personal safety] but instead a society torn apart: where since 1960 violent crime has increased 550% and the illegitimacy rate has soared to 30% from 5% and where today one child in eight is raised on welfare. The social problems of the West make us wonder about the term 'Asian values'. What has brought Asia its newfound wealth is not the discovery of some mythical set of new principles, but its faithful adherence to the old verities: hard work, enterprise, family thrift,

> responsibility. Today these values may be called 'Asian', but in essence they are also the protestant work ethic, or Victorian virtues that helped build the West. The difference between Asia and the West is that Asia still respects the universal values that many in the West no longer seem to cherish."[4]

The European company representative about to take up an expatriate position in Asia is likely to find the task of understanding Asians daunting. Asians comprise 60 per cent of the world population; there are five major cultures, three major religions (Confucianism, Islam, and Hinduism), and countless forms of social organization. But by focusing on the particular host country, and with a willingness to learn, such obstacles can be overcome in time. Viewed from Europe Southeast Asia seem to be a relatively homogeneous group of countries. This perception reinforces the European "view" about Asia, developed in Europe. But when the European actually visits and/or works in ASEAN countries he or she realizes that Southeast Asia is in fact one of the most diverse regions in the world. These diversities have a direct impact on different management styles which to the inexperienced European manager will be simply baffling.

> "Antonio Lopez, a management consultant at the Asian Institute of Management in Manila, says that the differences between ASEAN countries' approaches to management are arguably greater than those between individual ASEAN countries and other parts in Asia. Singapore's stress on organization and discipline, for example, is guaranteed to chime well with Japan's style of corporate management. While the Philippines' more innovative—and perhaps, more hedonistic—approach to life usually sits comfortably with expatriate American managers."[5]

Through daily interaction with local partners and staff, the expatriate manager will become aware of the emphasis placed on, and the resources invested in, the protection of Asian values. Children are taught these values from a very early age: in Korea, they spend two hours a week learning about the "26 virtues"; Taiwanese children are taught "moral education" for 40 minutes a week; and Singaporean children are instructed in moral values in their mother tongue. Unless foreign managers can show through their deeds that they respect such values, quality performance, as assessed by their Asian partners, will be difficult to achieve. If they have not gained an understanding of the underlying culture, then no amount of knowledge of rules and regulations will compensate.

The following eight basic values in Chinese culture are found throughout Southeast Asia:

1. *A sense of history*
   This value is based on a strong sense of one's long cultural heritage and place in the scheme of things. Reverence for one's ancestors, and a sense of responsibility to one's children and the community, are deeply rooted in Asian cultures. The path to self-realization is through offering one's services to others. The self and society are considered as an integral whole.
2. *A sense of transcendence and immanence*
   "Uphold what is righteous without calculating its benefits and follow the Way regardless of the results," said Tung Chung-shu in the 1st century BC. "The Way" is a set of principles to be adhered to in life that transcend personal gains or losses. In order to transcend worldly considerations, one cultivates detachment from personal success.
3. *The pursuit of self-discipline*
   The battle to be waged is not with society, as in Western thought, but with oneself. Self-indulgence is considered a negative trait, while self-discipline is respected. Self-discipline does not begin with social interaction. "Clearing away the bandits in the mountains is easier than clearing away the bandits in one's own heart," said the 15th century neo-Confucian scholar Wang Yang-ming. There is a strong belief in Asian cultures in man's own spiritual resources, unlike in the secular value system of the West.
4. *Acceptance of authority*
   Authority is accepted willingly rather than as a legal obligation. For the traditional Chinese, the five cardinal objects of adoration were heaven, the earth, political authorities, and one's forefathers and teachers. Although these values have been accused of being feudal and hindering social progress, and the ritualistic aspects have been

abolished, the political, family, social, and intellectual authorities are still revered.

5. *The unimportance of material things*
   Although Confucius enjoyed food, music, and dancing, in the Confucian tradition "A man of virtue will be at ease under whatever material conditions." This stems from the notion that all material things—fame, social status, and so on—are things external, which are secondary to things internal. China's turbulent history has taught its people that all things external are like passing clouds, and that it is pointless to become attached to them. One's spiritual tranquillity does not rest on the satisfaction of one's wants. As the ancient Chinese philosopher Chuangtze observed, "He that is absorbed in the pursuit of his own interests will have little celestial fire." This doesn't mean that one should exercise asceticism, but rather that one should be content with having one's basic needs met, not one's wants satisfied.
6. *Happiness lies in dedication*
   In the 2nd century AD, Zhuge Liang, a respected man of learning, taught his son, "In transcending material gains, one's dedication manifests itself and in quietude one's way persists." This is the spiritual happiness to which Confucians aspire. It is evident in the Asian aesthetic taste in painting, which admires beauty in simplicity.
7. *Continuity of the family*
   In most Asian societies, the meaning of life is derived to a large extent from the family tree. This doesn't simply mean caring for one's parents and rearing one's children. As Mencius, a sage of the 3rd century BC, said, "Many claim credit or filial piety for having looked after their parents. But if one looks after the dog and horses in the same way, how much will looking after one's parents be worth?" Nursing one's parents without reverence and love means little. Filial piety requires that one follows the way of the father, as Confucius taught: "Following the way of one's deceased father for three years may be considered as filial piety." This value is still upheld by many Chinese today as a way of maintaining social stability.
8. *Comparing without judging*
   Value systems derive from a society's economic, social, and

> intellectual history. They should be judged only on their ability to maintain a full and harmonious relationship between the individual and society. Comparison is meaningful only when it enables us to learn from others' experience.

It is essential that Europeans doing business in Asia try not to impose their own standards, norms, and values on the host culture. On the issue of human rights, for example, unless we attempt to understand the Asian point of view, we will continue to go around in circles. Instead of emphasizing development aid in budgetary appropriations, economic co-operation should be fostered. What Asians want is not to be given a product but taught how to make it for themselves. The key is self-sustainability. The private sector plays a key role in creating an environment of self-sustainability, and private companies in Southeast Asia are looking for partners with whom to develop trusting partnerships with common goals.

The rising power of Asia can be attributed to the fusion between Eastern and Western values that has occurred in the region in the second half of the 20th century. The thirst for knowledge has enabled Asians not only to acquire a greater knowledge of Europe than Europe has of Asia, but also to apply it, through a process of syncretism, in their own development. In the process, a sense of community is emerging that has made Asia the most dynamic region in the world. As Kishore Mahbubani, Permanent Secretary of Singapore's Ministry of Foreign Affairs, identified in an article entitled "The Pacific Way",[6] Asians are confident that their moment in history has come, and that it is well-earned. They are determined to maintain their "miracle growth" through co-operative partnerships with the West in the areas of technology, know-how, and cross-border capital. The new Asian culture that is emerging is soundly based on Eastern values, but with an understanding of and familiarity with Western culture. The new Asians are a blend of East and West, and they are showing the rest of the world the way forward into the 21st century.

## CONCLUSION

Asians see their cultural differences as a competitive advantage, as an asset rather than a liability. Through adopting the approach of "unity in diversity", they have achieved enormous success in promoting growth and development in the region by non-institutionalized means. Asia is fast being developed by the Asians themselves, on their own terms. If Europeans continue to react defensively to Asian competition instead of investing in those markets, they will become obsolete in the Asian—and, by extension—the global market-place. But in order to form effective partnerships in Asia, European businesses will have to undergo a critical switch in attitude from the short term to the long term. They will need to plan integrated regional business strategies, research the needs of the local markets, and select and train managers who are sensitive to issues of cross-cultural communication. Nowhere is this need for empathy with the local culture more apparent than at the negotiating table. In the next chapter we consider the issues arising from negotiating in a cross-cultural context in some detail.

Appendix no. 4 compares European and Asian management styles. Appendix no. 5 uses a brushstroke approach in identifying broad categories of similarities and differences between European and Asian cultures.

## ENDNOTES

[1]Colin Randlesome, *Business Cultures in Europe*, Butterworth Heinemann, Oxford, 1993.
[2]*The Economist*, 20 May 1995, p. 90.
[3]From *Eurobusiness*, March 1995, p. 121. Reproduced by permission.
[4]*Far Eastern Economic Review*, 23 June 1994, p. 5.
[5]The London *Financial Times*, 4 December 1995, p. 12.
[6]Kishore Mahbubani, "The Pacific Way", *Foreign Affairs*, January/February 1995, pp. 100–111. This article appeared in *Foreign Affairs*, 1995, by the Council on Foreign Relations, Inc.

# 5
# Negotiating in a Cross-cultural Context

## INTRODUCTION

A seed planted in the earth will not grow if it is not properly watered. In the same way, negotiations of European–Asian joint ventures cannot be expected to bear fruit without the sound management of cross-cultural communication issues and problems. Much has been written about negotiating skills in business. For instance some analysts concluded that courses in negotiating skills are highly beneficial. So often business people meet resistance at the negotiating table and cannot find a way through. Especially when working with Asian business people, an ability to gain their confidence and respect requires patience and conciliation.

The ultimate challenge in successfully negotiating a European–Asian joint venture or other agreement leading to international technology transfer lies in creating a triangle of negotiations–transactions–negotiations. This chain implies an attitude of adaptability, since the philosophy of "create to innovate" requires the European partner to adjust to the host country's culture. Hence, cross-cultural—both national and corporate—communication is at the heart of negotiations and thus provides the focus of this chapter.

# A HISTORICAL PERSPECTIVE ON CROSS-CULTURAL NEGOTIATIONS IN SOUTHEAST ASIA

European companies looking to invest in the emerging Asian markets need to be aware of how those countries have historically viewed foreign companies' involvement in their development process. Two main periods can be identified in the evolution of the Asian perspective: the period of confrontation (the 1950s to the mid-1970s), and the period of co-operation (mid-1970s to the present).

During the period of confrontation, the developing countries were sensitive to the threat of economic domination by foreign-based transnational companies. Their uneasiness about possible exploitation of their resources was compounded by doubts about the overall contribution such companies could make to their economic development. Thus, although investment incentives were provided to foreign companies, policies were designed to minimize the control they could exercise over the local economy. Many of the developing countries enacted legislation requiring a majority of local equity in foreign enterprises, a high proportion of locals in top positions, increased foreign exchange earnings, and a reduction of imports of raw materials and spare parts. They attempted to apply these policies uniformly and on a non-discriminatory basis to all foreign companies, which led to breakdowns in the negotiations process. Furthermore, sectors considered of vital national importance — such as transportation, communications, public utilities, raw materials extraction, and certain manufacturing industries — were declared off-limits to foreign investors.

From the mid-1970s there was a marked shift in the relations between foreign companies and the authorities in the developing countries. Government policies which had been protective and regulatory now promoted a spirit of openness, deregulation, and privatization. Foreign transnational companies were no longer perceived as capitalist–imperialist agents of their home governments but as organizations with appealing economic attributes. In the last decade or so, foreign companies have emerged in certain specific sectors (for example, in the banking, mining, and petroleum industries in Singapore, Malaysia, Indonesia, and Thailand); local high-tech skills have been developed (in microelectronics in Singapore, and aircraft and shipbuilding in Indonesia); and new policies, rules, and regulations have been designed to maximize the presence of foreign companies in the region.

The changes that have taken place in recent decades are the result of a long process of adaptability on the part of host country governments, local firms, and foreign transnational companies, dating back to the colonial era. Researchers who have observed the performance of foreign companies in the developing Asian markets over the years have developed two schools of thought on their role in the region. One school sees the foreign companies as a commanding influence: so powerful are they in political terms that they can initially dictate to the host country the terms of investment as spelled out in tax incentives, investment allowances, repatriation of profits, and a host of other facilities related to foreign direct investment policy. This school emphasizes lobbying and other forms of political manipulation as essential aspects of the negotiation process. On the other hand, there are those who maintain that foreign transnational companies are passive victims of a bewildering and continually tightening web of bureaucratic controls offering few alternatives. Both schools acknowledge the direct impact that foreign transnational companies have had, and continue to have, on local firms in the emerging markets. These three periods of confrontation, co-operation and adaptation are visually presented in Appendices 6–8.

In the 1980s, for example, foreign direct investment in the ASEAN countries, with the exception of the Philippines, more than doubled. During the same period, Japan, Taiwan, Singapore, and Korea built up substantial exchange reserves in US dollars, which led to an increase in foreign direct investments. Wage rates, land costs, and the skills base in some Southeast Asian countries grew relative to those in countries like the United States and Canada. These changes led to a marked shift in the comparative advantage of some countries, and thus to relocation of some low-cost production. Foreign direct investment from countries in the region has increased, and is largely concentrated within the region. Likewise, foreign direct investment from Indian, Pakistani, and other Asian firms in Britain is concentrated in Asia via joint ventures with local companies. While the two-way flow of foreign direct investment has accelerated world-wide, and is now considered the rule, a remarkable new trend is the entry on the scene of lower-income countries such as Indonesia and Malaysia. For example, locally-owned firms in Indonesia are accessing products and process technology, as well as management expertise, from abroad via foreign direct investment in high-income markets. Singapore, Taiwan, and Korea have all successfully expanded their output, exports, and employment levels.

Joint ventures in Southeast Asia require perseverance, patience, and hard work. What might be thought a wise decision in the short term may turn out to be a very bad one in the long term. For example, Uniroyal was engaged in a joint venture with an Indonesian company making latex for rubber gloves, condoms, and balloons. The market had not materialized as quickly as Uniroyal had hoped, and it sold its interest to the local partner. Within months, the AIDS epidemic exploded publicly and the demand for condoms—and latex rubber—skyrocketed.

A long-term, patient approach was taken by Singapore, where General Electric and Philips each employed over 10 000 people in the production of radios, small domestic appliances, and television sets. The Singapore government provided all the necessary incentives to ensure the success of the venture. However, it also nurtured Singapore's technological self-reliance by training its own people and providing them with the capability to develop the technology themselves. As a result, Singapore is today—along with Taiwan, Korea, Hong Kong, and India—considered a strategic country not only from the point of view of individual foreign transnational companies, but also in world business. The country's investment in creating an indigenous, high-tech microelectronics industry, and massive training and management programmes, has paid off.

In Malaysia, forecast to become an industrialized country by 2020, a key factor is the appropriate development of its human resources. Consequently, foreign management and information consulting companies are playing a significant role in technology transfer. For example, the total market for consultancy services in Malaysia increased by 10–12 per cent per year between 1989 and 1993, or about the same rate of growth as the national economy. Americans and the British (the latter largely for historical reasons) have a strong presence in the consulting sector, which is likely to consolidate the position of certain sectors of the local population.

Early collaborative arrangements in Malaysia were largely with local Chinese firms, which were dominated by Chinese—rather than Malay or Indian—technicians and managers. This arose not from any cultural bias on the part of the foreign partner, but from the predominance of the Chinese in the economic affairs of the country as a result of their historical association with retail outlets and distribution networks throughout Malaysia. The Malaysian government intervened by implementing its "Bhumiputra" (sons of the soil) policy, which requires all foreign companies to increase the equity holdings of Malay nationals and fixes quotas according to the ethnic groups employed by the organization.

Asian governments, aware that a successful joint venture requires a disciplined work-force, have taken steps to curb the effective power of trade unions and to ensure a positive climate for foreign direct investment. The very few studies that have been carried out on the performance of foreign transnational companies in Southeast Asia indicate the positive impact of joint ventures on the development of local entrepreneurship. The impact of foreign companies on the host country can generally be ascribed to four factors: the level of industrialization of the host country, the sectors of the economy in which the foreign company operates, the integration of those sectors with the rest of the national economy, and the policies of the host country government. Some researchers in international business strategies concluded that:

1. Ventures are more successful where partners are related (in products, markets and technologies) horizontally than when they are vertically related or unrelated to their ventures;
2. Ventures last longer between partners of similar cultures, asset sizes and venturing experience levels;
3. Ventures last longer when their activities are related (in products, targets and technology) to both of its sponsors' activities.[2]

When developing countries were experiencing a debt crisis there was a growing realization that the international debt/equity ratios of many of those countries were seriously out of balance, even despite the debt crisis. Many developing countries discovered that their level of international debt put them at risk of losing control over their economies and economic policies. The World Bank, acting on behalf of their creditors, imposed requirements that exceeded their worst fears regarding loss of control to foreign transnational companies. During the same period, a number of developing countries, including many in Southeast Asia, implemented export promotion policies.

Transnational companies generally resent the imposition of regulations and restrictions. Some countries have successfully designed and implemented very stringent regulatory and benefit-sharing policies and yet have been able to attract foreign investors, while others with generous incentive programmes have found it difficult to attract investment. The former countries generally have plentiful resources, high indigenous production capacity, and large markets, while the latter tend to be smaller and more backward.

Technological developments over the last few decades have prepared the ground for an increasingly transcultural and competitive world. Hand-in-hand with the internationalization of business goes cross-cultural communication and the need for a learning culture in businesses operating in the global market-place. Knowledge shared is not knowledge lost; rather, the general knowledge base is enlarged and is quickly communicated around the world. However, the barriers to communication may prevent the spread—and thus the accumulation — of knowledge. Cross-cultural communication is therefore increasingly a core concern in the world today.

Although perseverance, patience, and hard work are the essential ingredients in any successful joint venture, first the partners must sign a joint venture agreement, which necessitates their sitting down and negotiating the terms of their partnership. The negotiating process requires adaptability to the local culture. Each country in the region poses its own particular challenges to the prospective foreign partner. A country-specific, rather than a regional, business strategy is required for negotiating with host country governments and local companies. In the next section we consider more closely the cross-cultural negotiation process.

## THE CROSS-CULTURAL NEGOTIATION PROCESS

Competing for a share of the Kuala Lumpur or Bangkok markets is no different from competing in New York or Rome: one must protect one's brand, choose an appropriate specialization or diversification strategy, and form a team comprising the best available professionals. That is why the APEC–Asem–WTO dialogue could — if successfully concluded — create great benefits of businesses thus, the question lies not in *what* to negotiate, but *how* to negotiate.

### How to Negotiate

Three factors influence negotiations. The first is the alliance between the foreign company and the host country firm. This includes the objectives of both parties, the duration of the alliance, and the number of business functions, products, and markets. It also encompasses the degree of uncertainty surrounding the activities of the alliance as a result of the attitudes and actions of competitors, local customs, and unpredictable government agencies, as well as the competence of the host country firm and its familiarity with the task at hand.

A second factor is the organizational complexity of the local firm and the degree of responsibility of local personnel for implementing decisions. Finally, the issue of cultural differences, and the cultural expectations Asians have of Europeans, must be considered. For example, Germans and the British have a reputation for being punctual, while Italians and the Spanish are regarded as being more casual about time. Differences such as these can result in serious misunderstandings and may impact on deadlines. The French tend to focus on general principles, while the English are more interested in identifying the practical implications. Germans typically are concerned with the impact of a problem on other aspects of the operation, such as associated processes.

These attitudinal differences among Europeans produce markedly different behavioural patterns. In Germany, information is coded and transmitted formally, there are no sharp distinctions between those inside and outside the culture, and changes are brought about relatively easily, quickly, and efficiently. This behaviour contrasts with the British, who tend to internalize and imply information, and to maintain strong bonds and a clearer distinction between insiders and outsiders. Their cultural patterns are well-entrenched and resistant to change. Consequently, Germans tend to use the "hard sell" approach, while the British rely on understatement and a "soft sell" approach.

The highly compartmentalized cultures of Europe contrast sharply with the need in the global market-place, and Southeast Asia in particular, for a unified and decisive European voice. This lack of co-ordination is nowhere more evident than at the international negotiating table.

We shall now review some of the main ingredients of the cross-cultural communication process. Clearly, it plays a critical role around the negotiating table, where the soundness of any approach to negotiations is put to the test. At the negotiating table, interpersonal communication is the key activity guiding negotiators on opposite sides of the table through moves, counter-moves, concessions, and reactions. Both parties communicate and receive verbal and non-verbal messages providing vital information on intangible as well as tangible issues. Successful negotiations depend upon an awareness that they are only the starting-point of a long-term process of developing an empathy for the culture of the host country and adapting one's behaviour to it. They rely on the awareness of the possibility of misunderstandings arising between the parties due to real or imagined cultural differences, and the associated expectations about behaviour. And particularly in Asia, both parties must ensure that neither loses face, or the negotiations will be doomed from the start.

A vast quantity of literature on how to negotiate international business deals has been generated by practitioners, academics, and analysts. The following discussion draws on that fund of knowledge, as well as on my personal experience in negotiating in Southeast Asian markets.

The work that goes into preparing to negotiate is aimed at eliciting a positive response from the prospective host country partner. If this is successful, negotiations will proceed to the "face-to-face" bargaining stage. Hence, the soundness of the preliminary negotiating work is all-important. For example, to ensure that contact is made at the right level, European business people setting up meetings with prospective Asian partners should ensure that their name cards give a translation of their job title and an indication of their seniority. Women should also ensure that their card indicates their gender. Attention to this kind of detail is important to Asian business people, who risk losing face if the negotiators are not evenly matched. A sound negotiating strategy based on total communication will provide answers to such questions as:

- how to proceed from the opening statement to concrete proposals—that is, bargaining;
- how to move from proposals to counter-proposals;
- how to make concessions without losing face or strategic advantages;
- how moves and counter-moves, proposals and counter-proposals, can be integrated into and presented during the final decision-making phase;

- how to move from a verbal agreement to a written agreement while complying with the regulations and laws of the host country;
- how to ensure that the verbal and written agreements reflect the legal interpretations of both parties; and
- how to meet the prospective partner's expectations that greater weight will be given to the verbal agreement than to the written agreement, especially in countries such as Indonesia where modern corporate labour law makes no consideration for the needs of management.

A total communication system involves five aspects of communication—verbal, non-verbal, situational, contextual, and social—aimed at understanding not only what is said but also what is meant. The verbal aspect is the language used around the negotiating table. English is a frequent choice, because it provides an international neutral ground since it is a foreign language for most continental Europeans as well as for Asians, with the exception of Singaporeans and Filipinos. Conducting negotiations in the local language through interpreters may prove awkward, particularly if the interpreter is a member of the local team. The best approach is for the European negotiators to converse in the language of the host country. This puts the potential Asian partner at ease, because it reduces the risk of their making mistakes and losing face in front of their colleagues. It also shows that the European representatives have done their homework and gone some way towards assimilating the local culture which is implicit in its language. Even if they are not proficient, their efforts will be well received. When Tony Miller, Director-General of Trade in Hong Kong, held his year-end briefing in Cantonese in December 1994, he became the first expatriate official to hold a press conference in Cantonese. Mr Miller impressed many who watched him on television explaining difficult trade issues in the local language. He is now going a step further, catching up with the tide of change engineered by the takeover of Hong Kong by China in 1997, and learning Putonghua (Mandarin). When asked about his attempts to master these difficult languages, he replied: "I don't like to be treated as a *heung ha chia* [country bumpkin] when addressing Beijing."

While it may be preferable to conduct the verbal negotiations in the language of the Asian party, the same is not true of the written agreement. In most Asian languages, the written word is not a literal representation of the spoken word. Thus, misunderstandings can arise from reliance by the European party on documents that have been translated. In any case, most Asians prefer informal agreements on the main points, because they regard litigation arising from disputes as to the interpretation of formal documents as a threat to harmony.

Of even greater importance than the language used is, of course, what one says and how one says it. There are five key stages in the negotiation process. In the first stage, after the preliminary courtesies and the formal presentations have been concluded, the floor passes to the European representative to begin the bargaining strategy. The most important thing is to create a good first impression, and this is achieved not so much by what one says as by how one says it. The delivery must reflect the local culture by adopting a "soft sell" approach. The foreign negotiator should avoid creating the impression of being unyielding, either through the speed, pitch, or intonation of his or her voice or their body language. The most important message to get across is a willingness to negotiate, and this is transmitted as much through non-verbal means of expression as verbal means. For the Asian partner, the reality is what they perceive, not what has been said or intended.

In Southeast Asia, expressions of emotion are frowned upon, and hence both verbal and non-verbal language can easily be misunderstood. As many analysts have explained, "Over-familiarity must be avoided. Formal politeness and emotional restraint are imperative." Asians tend to react to messages perceived to be rude, belligerent, or sarcastic by acting in a way that reduces their loss of face in front of their peers. Unless the European team is well acquainted with the host country, they will be unaware that such a reaction has even taken place, let alone be able to correctly interpret it.

When the host country team reacts to the opening gambit of the European team, the balance of power is established. The negotiations then turn to the second stage of identifying objectives, making initial offers and proposals, and seeking clarification, followed by agreement on the course of action. This is the bargaining stage, where the main emphasis is on interaction between the parties and the assimilation of information. Both parties spell out their respective positions on potentially divisive issues or problems. An impersonal power relationship develops: both parties test each other's limits and then try to accommodate the other's position. This process requires sound interpersonal, cross-cultural communication using verbal language to solve practical problems. Their positions are spelled out, and the conditions each party is prepared to accept are slowly clarified. More tea and rice cake may be served, and in the less formal atmosphere this generates it is appropriate to use phrases such as: "Could we ask you a question? What if . . .?" and "If we could make a suggestion: provided that you could . . . we might . . ." This "softly softly" approach gives the hosts time to clarify their own earlier proposals or statements, to consult with the rest of their team, and to have comparatively informal one-on-one contact. It also avoids confrontation, because no one feels compelled to express disagreement.

The entire process is geared to creating harmony, the axis around which social interaction rotates. If the potential Asian partners do not perceive harmony as the goal of the foreign company, then it will be virtually impossible to make any real progress at the negotiating table. Harmonious relations help to avoid confrontation and loss of face. Both parties are involved in articulating, shaping, and responding to behaviour in a spirit of determined co-operation and harmony, reflecting the local culture. This mutually supportive behaviour can also be a means to draw the host party out of its natural reserve, either to further encourage the foreign party's co-operation or to seek information. If representatives of European companies have learned that in Southeast Asia they negotiate a relationship not contracts they will know what attitudes to apply in this phase.

The succession of moves and counter-moves leads to the third negotiating stage, where further information is gathered, ambiguities are clarified, and problems are solved. Its purpose is to explore how the parties might reach a mutually beneficial agreement. During this stage, the relationship between the two parties changes. The European team may have to report to headquarters in Europe on the state of the proceedings, who may have little understanding of the host culture and be impatient to clinch the deal. It is up to the European team to form a communication "bridge" between headquarters and the Asian delegation. During this delicate transitional stage, moves and counter-moves are characterized by concessions. There are fears of loss of position in the negotiating process, and of loss of face in front of both the opposing and one's own team members. The questions asked during this phase will be probing in nature: "It would seem that we agree to . . . Is this your understanding?" "Do we understand you correctly . . . ?" Speech is characterized by pauses between sentences and between one party's contribution and the response of the other party. Pauses are perceived as taking time to consider the other's viewpoint. Malaysians, Indonesians, and Thais typically pause longer before speaking than do Europeans, who may interpret silence as awkward or embarrassing, as a sign of confusion or prevarication, or as a negative response instead of simply as a culturally acceptable mode of interaction in the host society. Interrupting suggests to the Asian side that the European representative considers their views unworthy of consideration. This could erase any initial favourable impression. The European team should resist the temptation to fill gaps with meaningless chatter, as this will cause offence to the host.

Cultural differences are also apparent in the area of eye contact. Asian cultures frown on over-reaction and public displays of emotion. Thus, they tend to avoid extended eye contact, considering it an over-reaction, whereas in the West eye contact is usually considered an important part of non-verbal communication which confirms or modifies what is being said. Europeans unfamilar with Asian cultures may perceive Asians' reluctance to maintain eye contact as a sign of shiftiness. A further issue is the projection of a desired image of oneself. When contradictory signals are received, through verbal and non-verbal behaviour, this may suggest to an Asian negotiator that a false image is being presented. In some parts of Asia, the leader of the host team may prefer to remain silent and let another person in the team lead the discussion. The fact that this person has been chosen (because of their language ability, say) to play a more powerful role in the negotiations, and in the eyes of both his or her peers and superiors in the organization and the European team, is significant. It is important, therefore, not to sidestep the delegate and address the actual leader instead.

Given these various differences, there is a real danger at this stage that if the European team members don't adapt their behaviour to the culture of the host country, they may alienate the Asian team.

An essential difference between European and Asian corporate cultures that also might have a negative impact on negotiations is the concept of loyalty. Asian firms tend to prioritize goals such as steady employment and other socio-cultural factors over profits. Differences such as these will emerge in the course of the negotiations and must be resolved to the satisfaction of the Asian partner. This applies also to the timing of their agreement. After weeks of negotiations, the European team will be impatient to conclude the discussions, while the Asian view is that time is not a commodity, like money, but eternal. This ties in with the problem of expectations. Real expectations are usually never spelled out, so a gap develops between expressed and unexpressed expectations. Europeans prefer to spell out their expectations clearly, and are usually under pressure from shareholders to make short-term decisions aimed at making an immediate profit. In Asia, the relationship between business and government is much closer than in the West. As the government exerts considerable control over bank funding of expansion projects, the host company's ability to finance long-term business strategies, with the additional bargaining power that this implies, should not be underestimated by the Europeans.

Another important aspect of expectations is the personal expectations of the individuals involved. Europeans operate within company systems based on achievements and rewards. They will be looking for compensation, in the form of bonuses or promotions, if they clinch the deal. They will have to justify their expenses on their return to Europe, which may contribute to their mounting impatience.

Finally, there is the issue of consensus. The host country spokesperson might need to discuss matters in private with his or her team where the culture encourages group consensus in decision-making. Any resulting delays should not be perceived as deliberate procrastination or a lack of interest. Asians are shrewd negotiators, and the goal of consensus is aimed at preserving harmony and friendship—that is, social obligations come before business. This is reflected in the general absence of modern company and contract law in Asia. Asian business executives are more interested in contracts as a basis for relationships with their partners than as legal documents. Thus, time is required at this stage of the negotiations to merge the European and Asian approaches and so reach a mutually agreeable position.

Three different approaches are commonly recognized in the literature on relationships: the psychodynamic approach, the cognitive approach, and the role theory approach. In the psychodynamic approach, one's personality and life history are considered the central determinants of one's relationships with others. The cognitive approach emphasizes interpretation and understanding as key elements in one's relations with others, while the role theory approach interprets people's relationships on the basis of the specific roles they play. In the context of the cross-cultural negotiating process, the most appropriate approach to take is based on cognitive theory.

The wide gap between European and Asian ways of thinking has a dramatic impact on negotiations. Only if the Europeans can share the assumptions of the team sitting across the table from them, can they build a sound relationship. Only mutually satisfactory interaction will produce the desired outcome. Assumptions are embedded in one's thought structures and world view. Business is part of this view, but, as stated earlier, in the Asian view friendships and social obligations come before business. Emphasis is placed on long-term, not short-term, results. Consequently, deadlines are considered as flexible and non-restrictive. Results are achieved not by the individual but by their closely woven social network, in which the needs of the extended family and the group are the prime motivating factor.

Both individual and group behaviour are determined by issues of pride and conformity. Without face-saving measures, there can be no interpersonal relationships. These relationships form a network of obligations characterized by patronage and nepotism which permeate society and social organizations. Cognitive processes—that is, the way people think—are characterized by intuition and sensual data, sensitivity to context and relationships, and concern for reconciliation, harmony, balance, and face saving.

Business negotiations are seen as an opportunity to elicit as much technical information as possible, to test the relationship before agreeing to be friends, to acquire essential information in order to avoid losing face, to assimilate data and technical information and be able to understand how these diverse elements fit into the system as a whole, thus maintaining harmony while eliciting change. The Asian team may require the European team to present technical seminars in order to learn about technical matters in greater depth. All of these factors explain any apparent procrastination on the part of the Asian negotiating team.

To the European, time is a perishable commodity; time is money. High priority is given to scheduling and deadlines. A certain amount of time is allocated for negotiations when the team makes its initial approach to the prospective Asian partner, and their patience may start to wear thin as the proceedings bog down during this third stage. Europeans place high priority on meeting personal needs, which could act as a barrier to cross-cultural communication.

The above general differences between Europeans and Asians are compounded by the differences between individual European cultures and Asian cultures. Each combination of nationalities around the negotiating table will pose unique challenges in bridging cultural gaps.

The fourth stage of the negotiating process moves from problem-solving to exploring the implications of the agreed points, with a view to reaching an overall agreement on their partnership. If the European team has been able to view the process on the basis of the whole relationship rather than its parts, and the local team is satisfied that the proposed system is a harmonious blending of many diverse elements, then, given government approval, the negotiation can proceed to the final stage: signing the contract. The main issue to resolve here is whether the contract will reflect the detailed verbal agreement or simply summarize it, and the language in which it will be couched. Since the host country might not have enacted modern corporate legislation, if a future dispute between the parties were to go before an arbitration board or the courts, the ways in which the contract can be interpreted and the language used will become important issues.

Once the contract has been signed, the European partner should not hand over immediately to a junior partner. Written communications and personal visits should continue during the handover period, as Asian business people expect and enjoy continuity.

## Beyond the Negotiating Table

Once a joint venture company has been set up, the expatriate partner will be concerned with cross-cultural issues as they arise in the day-to-day operation of the venture. The general principles that applied during the negotiations will continue to apply in daily interaction with Asian partners and employees, as well as with government and other officials. As this book has stressed, they will play an important part in the eventual success or failure of the operation.

There must be more than token adjustment to the foreign culture, and ultimately learning must take place on both sides. In competing for a slice of the Asian market, European expatriate managers must be willing to adapt to local circumstances, to continue to adapt as required over the long term, and to apply the lessons learned in the process. Unless there is adequate management of cross-cultural communication issues, European companies will have no better chance of forging a productive long-term partnership in the region than any of their competitors seeking to operate in the same market.

# Part III
## CREATING EUROPE INC.

# 6
# Learning from the Past

## INTRODUCTION

The fast-growing and increasingly wealthy markets in Southeast Asia provide significant openings for foreign investors in the areas of high-technology, industrialization, basic infrastructure (water, power, transport, and telecommunications), consumer goods, and services such as health care, education, and technical and professional training. A superficial reading of European newspapers might give the impression that European businesses are already very active in the region. According to an article entitled "Britain: Eastward Ho!" in the *Sunday Telegraph* of 30 January 1994, "In the first 11 months of 1993 UK exports to the Asia Pacific region rose by 30 percent to £6.9 billion and imports by 28 percent to £10 billion." And on 29 November 1993, *Newsweek* carried a feature entitled "Pacific Overture" which made special reference to the "recent trip of German Chancellor Helmut Kohl to China—a trip during which, the *China Daily* reports, German firms signed more than 20 deals worth $2.8 billion." However, the European business person based in Asia is acutely aware that EU businesses are poorly represented in the region.

The reference framework in the region is not homogeneous. The area has a diverse range of cultures, religions, geography, demographics, history, and educational standards, all producing distinct national cultures. Nevertheless, distinct ethics and morals prevail in the region, with their emphasis upon respect for age and seniority, the avoidance of confrontation and loss of face, the importance of the group or community over the individual, and the cultivation of relationships based upon friendship and mutual respect. They are part and parcel of any business strategy.

Despite their poor record, many European companies are beginning to recognize the inadequacies of their business dealings with the emerging Southeast Asian markets and are looking to learn lessons from the past, as well as from the younger generation of business people who are more open to change, willing to be trained in and become better informed about Asian affairs, and sensitive to cultural nuances in cross-cultural communications. In this chapter we summarize the mistakes of the past, as discussed in Parts I and II, and in Chapter 7 we look at how Europe Inc. can put its house in order so as to be able to forge an integrated approach to investing in Southeast Asia. Chapter 8 considers the role of training in maximizing human resources as part of this process.

## THE ROLE OF EXPATRIATE MANAGERS IN SOUTHEAST ASIA

In Chapters 4 and 5 we examined the cultural differences between Europeans and Asians that can hinder communication at the grass-roots level of negotiating and implementing joint venture partnerships in the host country. The quality of European professionals in Asia does not, on the whole, compare favourably with that of their American and Japanese counterparts. They are not well informed about local policies and needs, and are less prepared to accept the shortcomings in the local systems (such as red tape, infrastructure problems, and lack of comforts) as constraints within which they have to work. The biggest problem in cross-cultural communication arises when foreign managers fail to adapt their ways of doing things to the local cultural and social environment. If they lack understanding, patience, a sound listening ability, and respect for the ways of others, they will both offend and alienate their actual or potential Asian partners. It is essential that European managers be aware of the actual and potential needs of Asians, as Asians perceive them, and not as European headquarters perceives them. The challenge for the expatriate manager is to act as a "bridge" between company strategists based in Europe and the end-users in Asia, so that investment policies can be adapted and modified to the long-term mutual benefit of both parties.

The expatriate manager must also consistently monitor the ever-changing policy environment of the Asian host country in order to be able to identify future opportunities. They must think strategically, with an appreciation of the long-term view of their local partners, while at the same time being able to react quickly to opportunities as they arise.

Most European managers based in Southeast Asia have been inadequately prepared for the job. Some analysts have estimated that as many as 30 per cent of European expatriates assigned to representative offices in the region quit before their time is up. Culture shock, false expectations, language and communication problems, difficult or unfamiliar living conditions, inadequate educational facilities for their children, the inability of their spouse to adapt to local conditions, stress, and an expatriate "ghetto" mentality contribute to this problem.

The ultimate success of a joint venture partnership will depend on the willingness and ability of the expatriate resident manager to overcome such problems and adjust to the local culture and values. He or she will need to reverse old ways of thinking and behaving: to replace individualism with group thinking, top-down decision-making with consensus, a short-term view with an eye on the long term, and a profit-orientation with a growth-orientation. A "best fit" between the European manager and the local environment is thus dependent upon the personal characteristics of the manager. Aspects of personal character that are relevant include cultural sensitivity, leadership style, adaptability, motivation, listening and management skills, career plans, health, a supportive family, flexibility, self-discipline, creativity, work patterns, personal philosophy, and language ability.

European expatriate managers must also be fully aware of their cultural strengths as Europeans. Their long history of cross-border commerce in Europe has given them an appreciation of and sensitivity to other cultures that their American counterparts, especially, lack. Asians see this as a strength, and it is one that is yet to be fully capitalized on by Europeans working in Asia. "Management in Palermo, Copenhagen, London, Paris or Frankfurt reflects different realities, to such an extent that one comes to the following apparently paradoxical conclusion: the identity of Europe is reinforced by combining diverse cultures."[1] Cultural diversity or flexibility makes it easier to perceive one's own characteristics and opinions as well as those of others; it ensures flexibility in the application of rules and values; and it supports creativity and impedes the impact of highly developed mass cultures. Cultural alertness helps in successfully managing brand portfolios in a global market.

All of the above comes down to the ability of the European manager to listen and be able to tune in to the needs of each of the links in the customer–supplier chain. A marketing orientation implies the ability to anticipate long-term trends by listening to actual and potential customers, local and expatriate employees, local Asian partners, and competitors. European negotiators are familiar with the sight of 15 or 20 Asian representatives sitting at the negotiating table, compared with five or six on the European side. The job of some of those 20 is simply to listen; only when the meeting breaks up do they take over. European managers would do well to adopt a similar strategy, which has enabled Japanese, Korean, Taiwanese, and other Asian businesses to correctly interpret cultural messages and establish successful business ventures in European countries.

## THE ROLE OF EUROPEAN HEADQUARTERS

There is a general lack of awareness of the actual requirements of the Southeast Asian markets, such as the need for the transfer and assimilation of "core" technology, and of the speed with which those markets operate. This has been partly due to cross-cultural communication problems, as well as to the failure to listen to, develop, and mobilize the expertise of human resources, both European and Asian.

European businesses need to learn that any economic co-operation strategy or programme has to be a two-way street where both partners can work together to achieve the chosen objectives. Europeans' reputation in Asia for talking rather than doing, their lack of awareness of Asian issues and values, and their fear of competition from Asia have all contributed to a policy of "conquering", rather than co-operating with, Asia in the business arena.

In *The Europe We Need*, Sir Leon Brittain said:

> "... Europeans do not always react to the irrepressible globalisation of the world economy with the boldness and vigour that it requires. Nowhere is this clearer than in our relations with Asia. A handful of relatively small nations in South-East Asia have rapidly grown into the most dynamic motor of economic growth in the world. Europe's consumers have given their cheap, high-quality goods a rapturous welcome, but many of Europe's companies are recoiling in fear, lobbying governments for protection rather than fighting back by competing on price, quality and service. The 'Tigers' of the Far East are to be kept at bay rather than challenged either in Europe's markets or on their own soil."[2]

In the past, transnational and medium-sized to small companies in Europe have taken a short-term view of their involvement in the Asian emerging markets. This is evident in the focus of belt-tightening measures when times are tough, such as cuts made to research and training budgets. They have failed to appreciate that investment in human capital will give the highest returns over the long term.

Headquarters of European companies often fail to provide the necessary support (in areas such as professional services, information and technological services, training, staffing, and timely responses) to their representatives operating in Asia, and attempt to exert direct control without understanding the challenges and problems faced by the manager on the spot. There is also inadequate screening, selection, and training of managers, and little thought given to planning their career path so that it capitalizes on their Southeast Asian experiences.

Experienced expatriates have a wealth of information that might usefully be employed by headquarters to adapt and modify their investment strategies. Recommendations made by "old Asia hands" include the following:

- Carry out an in-depth analysis of the local environment and market before the manager is installed.
- Concentrate on particular areas in order to reach a strategic critical mass.
- Lobby for the European Investment Bank to lend financial assistance.
- Develop a comprehensive intelligence network in the chosen country which will help to pinpoint suitable local partners and provide timely information thereafter.
- Research local business practices and adapt the company's investment strategy accordingly.
- Form strategic alliances in Europe.
- Develop a strategy for reacting quickly to the challenges and opportunities identified by the manager in the chosen market, in order to be able to compete with one's competitors.
- Co-operate with other European companies in continuously monitoring policies and developments in the chosen country.
- Adopt a pro-active approach in identifying local companies that are ripe for technological development, and develop services aimed at creating a market for existing products or services and/or the development of new ones in co-operation with the local company.
- Ensure that all relevant local institutions are consulted and included in the development framework.
- Assist the local host country government to develop long-term measures to foster R&D capabilities.
- Establish, in co-operation with the government, vocational training facilities, equipment, and financing. This will ensure the development of a pool of labour already skilled in European methods.

- Take advantage of the available institutional support in Europe. For example, European Union information centres can provide information on potential vendors in the chosen country and the services they can offer.

On 28 May 1995, the British newspaper *The Independent on Sunday*[3] published an article in their Inside Business section entitled "Learning by their biggest mistakes", by Michael Pearn, Tim Payne, and Chris Mulrooney of the firm of Pearn Kandola, chartered occupational psychologists based in Oxford, England, who help organizations to learn more effectively. The article contained the results of a survey carried out among 250 senior managers from a range of business sectors. The survey found that errors always occur in a particular context. The most common context (20 per cent of all mistakes reported in the survey) was in managing business expansion. The main lessons to be learned included the need to understand a country's culture before one can understand the way it approaches business. Companies were advised not to try and switch successful ideas from one culture straight into another, and that it is necessary to build allies if one wishes to bring about sustained change. Whatever the structure of the deal, personal relationships are always critical to its success. Companies should not underestimate the time and cost required to educate the market, and must never assume that things will improve of their own accord — one must make it happen. Managers should also never allow emotions to rule the pocket, and should not rely on the judgement of politicians, who, under pressure to be *seen* to perform, may be more concerned with short-term than long-term results.

## THE LACK OF A COLLECTIVE EUROPEAN VISION

Europe has failed, as yet, to develop and implement a penetration strategy for the Southeast Asian markets, unlike its competitors the United States and Japan. One reason for this has been the lack of government and institutional support, and the prioritizing — prior to Asem 1996 — of the Mediterranean and

Central European markets over Southeast Asia. Ventures into Asia tend to be in the form of forays by individual firms with an eye on the short-term rewards. There is a lack of both an individual and a collective vision. European industry can assert itself on the Asian and world stages only in partnership with others. In the preceding sections we examined this need for partnership in the context of individual firms co-operating with Asian joint venture partners. In this section, we consider the need for strategic alliances among, and the formulation of collective strategies by, European businesses and institutions.

The European Round Table of Industrialists (ERT) is an association of 45 major European industrial companies which express opinions on a number of crucial problems that concern politics as much as economics. With a combined turnover of some ECU 500 billion and more than three million employees, these companies have a significant impact on economic activity and employment in Europe. Members of the ERT have a specific interest in the developing world, whose market size was estimated in 1990 to exceed US$4 trillion (or two-thirds of the GNP of the European Union). Recent surveys by the ERT, which considers market dynamics and trends as more important than market size, examined conditions for investment in 25 developing countries in the period 1982–92 and analysed the impact of improved conditions for foreign direct investment on levels of investment. (Appendix no. 9 gives a summary of this survey.) Between 1980 and 1990, the European Community's share of OECD countries' foreign direct investment in the developing world fell from 37 per cent to 12 per cent. The results of the surveys indicated that the move towards less-restrictive regulations and a stronger private sector in the developing markets, which included Indonesia, Malaysia, the Philippines, Thailand, and Vietnam, is creating significant gains in efficiency and, ultimately, competitiveness and wealth. New opportunities and challenges are emerging, to which European industry must respond.

The region offers different advantages to different types of industries. For some companies the main advantage is lower labour costs, while for others Southeast Asia offers easy access to a niche market. An estimated two-thirds of value added in goods and services produced world-wide is not tradable over long distances, so product concepts and other industrial know-how must be brought to where the consumers are. Other estimates indicate that 30 to 40 per cent of world trade is affected by various forms of protectionism, which can be overcome by foreign direct investment.

Globalization is another important issue: a corporation's presence in developing countries and regions with high economic potential is necessary because the latter have become relevant within the world market and are directly affecting industries' economies of scale. Originally, the pattern of flows of foreign direct investment primarily followed single countries' rates of return; however, the strategic concept of competitiveness in global markets is increasingly directing companies' allocations of new investment. Economic and political forces world-wide are expanding intra-regional flows of trade, investment, and labour, and encouraging regional approaches to problem-solving. The processes of globalization and regionalization have developed simultaneously and reinforced each other. In Southeast Asia, market-led regionalization has been outward-looking, based on regional complementarities of resources and creating, rather than hindering, regional market opportunities for firms outside the region.

European companies need to become more competitive in world markets. At the World Economic Forum held in Davos, Switzerland, in February 1994, strategies for bringing Europe out of recession were discussed by captains of industry from all over the European Union.

The delegates were unanimous in their agreement that, with our social costs, fiscal levels and trade unions, we Europeans risk being left out of the market-place. Europe has high-quality products, but they have to be sold. It is not acceptable that a Mercedes costs 40 per cent more than an American car. We have to be competitive. Therefore, we have to work more, and more efficiently... China alone has 1.2 billion people. If we do not sell to these markets, somebody else will. If we are not able to become more competitive, one day these very countries will flood us with their exports.

If European business was to survive the recession, it would need to make savage cuts in operating costs, including work-force levels, and establish new manufacturing operations and other ventures in the growing low-wage markets of Southeast Asia and Eastern Europe. The European Union member states must endeavour to gain an immediate foothold in those markets to enable the Union to become an international player. Furthermore, there was a need for political leadership in Europe. These sentiments were reiterated at the 1995 and 1996 Davos summits. Gatherings such as these only serve to justify the criticism that Europeans will talk of making changes, but do little to bring those changes into effect.

Europeans are generally ignorant of the unity attributed by Asians to the member states of the European Union. While they continue to see themselves as representatives of German, French, or British companies, Asians see them as *Europeans*, in the same way that they see Europe's main competitors in the region as Japanese and Americans. Hence, the potential that is implicit in forging an integrated European approach to conducting business on the Southeast Asian and world stages which would place Europe firmly alongside Japan Inc. and USA Inc. has been largely overlooked. The Asians find it perplexing that the EU member states have failed to achieve the unity of approach that would ensure them a substantial slice of the Asian pie, particularly since Asian business leaders have openly expressed their willingness to be courted by European companies. This lack of an integrated approach, the inability to speak with one voice, is evident in the current fragmented, incoherent market penetration strategies of most European companies in Southeast Asia, and their failure to customize their approach in the areas of organizational and financial engineering, and the flexibility of services and products offered.

There are some 500 think tanks in Europe working on Asian affairs, most of them small, scattered, and struggling to survive. Many are unaware of the others' existence, and there is no single publication drawing together the results of their research. Despite this lack of a private pan-European approach to collecting and disseminating information, some significant efforts have been made at the national level to develop an efficient network of research centres focused on Asia. Examples include the Association of South-East Asian Studies formed by the University of Hull, the British Academy Committee for South-East Asian Studies, and the British Association of South-East Asian Studies, in the United Kingdom; and the Nordic Associations of Asian Studies, South Asian Studies, and South-East Asian Studies, in Copenhagen. The partnership between the Südasien Institute at Germany's Heidelberg University and England's South-Asia Centre at Cambridge University held the first European conference on modern South Asian studies in 1960, and the Eurasia Institute in Paris, France has compiled a directory of contemporary Asian Research Centres in Europe. There is obviously, then, a need for a central computerized databank which could make available information about, and analysis of, current developments in Asia for the benefit of European companies with an interest in investing in the region. Could the European Federation of Industries play a role?

Most companies who have already set up operations with Asian partners are reluctant to share the practical experience and expertise they have gained on the ground in Asia by providing financial and other support to universities and management schools responsible for educating the next generation of managers. The current lack of a collective vision is providing an advantage to the United States, Japan, and other competitors and damaging Europe's credibility, particularly in Southeast Asia; hence it is seriously jeopardizing the future of Europe in world trade.

The vision required to forge the collective will and co-operative strategies which we have called "Europe Inc." must be developed both at home in Europe, through lobbying by transnational and medium-sized to small companies of government bodies (both national and regional) and trade institutions, as well as in the representative offices of European governments, the EU institutions and trade agencies in Asia. At present, European businesses lack a global view and an appreciation of the tools already available to them in planning co-operative ventures in Southeast Asia. Government and trade organizations provide inadequate support in the form of financing of consortia and other strategic alliances looking to do business in the region. For example, European Union institutions seem reluctant to give the European Investment Bank an assertive role in this respect. The governments of the EU member states have failed to clarify their intentions and co-ordinate their strategies, and to communicate these to the EU Commission. For its part, the European Union's steady and timely flow of market intelligence from its representatives in Southeast Asia is considered to be, by many businessmen, the result of a Eurocratic process accountable to no one rather than an entrepreneurial approach.

The problems identified here must be dealt with by all the parties involved, either directly or indirectly, in shaping Europe Inc.: individual transnational and medium-sized to small companies; the 15 European governments; European Union institutions; groups of industrialists such as the European Round Table; European expatriate managers operating in Southeast Asian host countries; and European officials and diplomats based in representative offices and embassies in the region. All Europeans must adopt a collective willingness to change from a "play safe" culture to a learning one if we are to shape and apply long-term strategies for effective partnerships in Southeast Asia and elsewhere. The need for an effective and efficient private lobbying organization, publicly accountable, able to act simultaneously at national and European regional levels and with the sole purpose of mobilizing the forces and resources needed to shape Europe Inc., is readily apparent.

## LEARNING FROM EUROPE'S COMPETITORS

European businesses will do well to study closely their competitors in the international business arena and learn from their achievements and mistakes. European businesses tend to take the attitude of sole operators and jealously guard market information from their "competitors", instead of sharing it with their peers, as Japanese and American companies are likely to do. Because they see themselves as operating alone, they also have inadequate intelligence-gathering resources.

A particular advantage for European companies operating in Southeast Asian countries is the anti-Japanese/American sentiment stemming from the pressure to agree to attractively packaged deals offered by Japanese and American companies which result in a loss of economic independence for the Southeast Asian partner. This sentiment has resulted in an increased interest in doing deals with Europe that preserve local independence while promoting essential infrastructure development.

European private investors are less schooled in the principle of mutual benefit than their American and Japanese counterparts, who fund training programmes and research institutes with a view to the long term. Not only does this investment help to assess and address skilled labour shortages in Southeast Asia, but it also solidifies the partnership through educating local staff in the use of Japanese or American equipment and business practices.

Europe's competitors in Southeast Asia are also more willing to consult with local institutions about their programmes or activities. The institutional framework in Asia is complicated, with different bodies having overlapping responsibilities. Patience is therefore required in working with government and other bureaucracies, but companies looking to sidestep this time-consuming aspect of doing business in Asia will reduce their overall competitiveness.

The focus in Asia is upon the transfer of "core" technology. European businesses are in a prime position to challenge the dominance of USA Inc. and Japan Inc. in this area, given Southeast Asians' dissatisfaction with their record in this essential area of development.

## CONCLUSION

The common denominator in all of the above is attitude: of the resident managers operating in an alien cultural environment; of headquarters towards their company's role and mode of operation in the emerging Southeast Asian markets; and of European business in general towards Europe's role in the world trade arena. If we Europeans are unable to change our attitudes, we will fail to become integrated into the world economy. We live in a transcultural world with a global economy. By accepting this as a positive challenge, we will increase our performance and assert the role of Europe in Southeast Asia. Through adopting the required strategic planning, organizational, financial engineering; the necessary flexibility in services; the indispensable adaptability to local cultures; co-ordination and political clout supporting the enhancement of Europe's image in Asia via a cross-cultural approach, we will appreciate that the "threats" posed by Asia are in fact opportunities.

## ENDNOTES

[1]European Round Table. Business Survey on Developing Countries 1984.
[2]Sir Leon Brittain, *The Europe We Need,* Hamish Hamilton, London 1994, p. 139.
[3]Independent on Sunday, 28 May 1995, Inside Business Section, page 14.

# 7
# Putting the House of Europe Inc. in Order

A creative European approach to doing business in Southeast Asia is long overdue, but the approach taken must be evolutionary, not revolutionary. It must focus on changing the current attitudes of EU companies towards both the emerging Southeast Asian markets and the role of Europe in a transcultural world and global economy. A symbolic new institutionalized beginning started in Bangkok at the March 1996 Asem summit. Yet the work of substance must begin both at private and public sector levels. In this chapter we look at the sweeping changes in attitude that are required in the areas of cross-cultural communication, organizational and financial engineering, service flexibility, strategic marketing, strategic alliances, and human resource management. We reiterate our case that it is essential for European businesses to maximize their knowledge of Asia, so as to be able to understand the impact of culture on economic co-operation, and to accurately assess their past successes and failures in Asia on a pan-European scale. A systematic approach is required to begin to put our economic house in order and to lay the foundations for a sound "marriage" between East and West business partners.

## CHANGING ATTITUDES

### Cross-cultural Communication

Cultural differences, in themselves, are never an obstacle to growth; we only make them so through a lack of understanding and adaptation. Thus, when a European from a Catholic or Protestant tradition attempts to do business with someone from a Buddhist, Muslim, or Confucian tradition, there is no inherent reason why their future prospects for success cannot be good. All that is required is to be able to organize the resources necessary to do business (such as human capital, market-oriented linkages, financial engineering, and so on) while giving due respect to the cultures of the parties involved. It follows that cultural fluency is critically important in doing international business. Representatives of European companies who have a clear picture of a business opportunity and the deal they wish to close will have little chance of doing so if they are unaware of what their potential partners value (that is, co-operation and harmony). Again, they are neither negotiating nor living by a contract, but a relationship and its soundness. Appendix no. 10 outlines some examples on how to approach cross-cultural communication issues and problems. Appendix no. 11 gives some tips on how to strategically plan the penetration into the Southeast Asian markets.

## Organizational and Financial Engineering

Organizational engineering is the building of an efficient and effective system of customer–supplier market-oriented linkages (both within and outside the firm) through which know-how in all its forms can flow freely, while financial engineering is the increasing demand from customers that suppliers should be able to identify sources of finance for the work required. European suppliers need to be able to respond to Asian demands for development finance, not least because finance holds the key to many of the potential opportunities available in the many sectors where European industry could play an assertive role in the Southeast Asian markets. If European companies are able to be actively involved in helping to provide finance to their actual or potential Asian clients, then they will provide a very effective way of increasing demand and making it more predictable. However, European companies cannot master financial engineering on their own. Like their American, Japanese, Korean, and Taiwanese counterparts have done, they must form partnerships with appropriate institutions, such as the European Investment Bank.

### Service Flexibility

Evidence suggests that European companies have been unable to offer flexibility of service to their actual or potential customers in Southeast Asia to the degree provided by their competitors in the region. That is, they have failed to become market-focused.

### Strategic Marketing

Many European companies' marketing efforts are ineffective because they operate on a case-by-case basis and lack a global market penetration focus. Companies which have made little effort to see issues from the Asian customer's point of view need to adopt a customer-orientation in their business dealings if they are to satisfy customers' wants and identify new opportunities.

### Strategic Alliances

Although various forms of strategic alliance exist in Europe between customers, suppliers, and financial institutions, they are not geared to operating in the Southeast Asian markets. Understanding the dynamics of collaborative inter-firm relationships is fundamental to understanding the potential markets of the region. In order to develop those markets, European companies have to understand, appreciate, and act upon the need for them to develop relationships, and not simply produce, distribute, and market products. Whether the company is a large transnational firm or a medium-sized or small firm, the underlying philosophy must be "collaborate to innovate".

## THE EUROPEAN CONSTRUCTION INDUSTRY (ECI): A CASE IN POINT

An interesting example which illustrates the above points is the European Construction Industry (ECI) in general, and the Société Européenne de Construction (SEC), a joint company set up in Belgium by Laing (UK), Dumez (France), NCC (Sweden) and Strabag (Germany), in particular. SEC is very active in Europe and the international market-place, but of interest to us here is the strategic plans it is developing to expand in the Southeast Asian markets, where its main competitors are Japan (construction contracts), the United States (advice, design, and project management), Korea, and Taiwan. If European companies such as SEC are to win market share in Southeast Asia, they will have to discard their individualistic approach and operate according to the unified "Inc." principle which has proved so effective for their competitors. In the past, they have been unable to do this because of their inability to manage organizational and financial engineering issues.

An important factor in the failure to form strategic alliances to date has been the size of ECI firms. While the average annual turnover of the Japanese company Shimizu in 1993 was ECU 28 billion and that of American Fluor Daniel/Bechtel was ECU 27 billion, turnover of the largest European construction company, the French Bouygues, was only ECU 9 billion. Thus, European companies think less in global management terms than in terms of exploiting short-term opportunities on a case-by-case basis, whereas the construction business in Southeast Asian markets demands a long-term approach.

ECI firms' performance is geared to very small returns in the short term, which conditions their decision-makers' ability to think strategically about international marketing and to plan over the long term. They are unfamilar with the Southeast Asian business scene and thus are unable to offer the flexibility of service provided by their competitors in the region. Their market penetration efforts are packaged at the national level, and there is neither a co-ordinated approach nor an appropriately designed European framework, with the possible exception of SEC. ECI companies still have to achieve bargaining power in international negotiations (which are by definition complex, multilateral, and multicultural) if they are to secure prestigious programmes and projects representing a significant slice of the US$3 trillion Southeast Asian economic pie.

When ECI companies tender for projects in Southeast Asia, they appear more concerned about beating other members of the ECI than their other international competitors. This is perplexing to their potential Asian partners, who have a clear appreciation of European companies' potential clout in the region if they were to adopt a unified "Inc." approach. Underlying this attitude is the perception of "risk", rather than "opportunity", which is evident in cost-cutting measures and the failure to see the maintenance of "listening posts" in the region as a sound investment. American and Japanese construction companies, on the other hand, see the value of maintaining sizeable marketing offices in the region, staffed by full-time professionals with decision-making authority and a brief to create business opportunities.

There is a lack of political and financial support of ECI firms by European governments or the European Union as a whole. This unwillingness to collaborate at a European level is reflected in the financial weakness of most ECI firms (although contractors in Germany, Spain, and France have managed to secure institutionalized links with industrial banks). Since the financing of infrastructure projects is today very complex, and contractors are increasingly expected to help find the finance for new construction, the lack of European-wide facilities hinders their effectiveness in the Southeast Asian markets.

Despite the excellent reputation in Asia of European know-how, these organizational and financial engineering problems, combined with the lack of both effective and creative management of ECI companies and a unified approach to doing business worldwide, provide a critical advantage to European companies' direct competitors in Southeast Asia.

The next section discusses various practical initiatives that might be taken by individual companies to overcome these problems.

A birds'-eye view of the structure of the European Construction Industry (ECI) is presented in Appendix no. 12. A comparative analysis of the European Construction Industry (ECI) in terms of similarities and differences in the 15 EU member states is presented in Appendix no. 13. A comparative bird's-eye view analysis of the ECI with the American and Japanese Construction industries is presented in Appendix no. 14. An outline of the ECI's strategy is presented in Appendix no. 15. An approach for the future competitiveness of ECI in Southeast Asia is schematically illustrated in Appendix no. 16.

## PRACTICAL INITIATIVES IN FORGING EUROPE INC.

### Strategic Planning

To maximize the great opportunities available in Asia, and minimize the risks of operating there, EU companies have to have an Asian vision to be effectively supported by a strategic plan. It implies they should concentrate on Southeast Asian countries first, instead of spreading themselves dangerously thin across the vast continent. The purpose of this strategically planned concentrated effort is to reach a critical mass. Once it has been achieved, then they can use their Southeast Asian base to expand to other parts of Asia.

They should unite to lobby effectively for having competitive finance made available. European Union companies should recognize that cross-border business dealings can be as thorny an issue as cross-border politics. It is essential to replace nationalism with regionalism. Europeans should see themselves first and foremost as Europeans. Protecting one's national interests in the short term leads to lost contracts in the long term. The pioneering and co-operative spirit of SEC, which enables costs to be reduced while better serving Asian customers through being able to offer sound financing packages, should be emulated. The European Investment Bank is potentially a powerful ally for companies wishing to apply the "Inc." principle by forging consortia in Europe able to compete effectively in Southeast Asia. The EU should master the will to renew its present very narrow involvement in Asia and expand it significantly.

To this purpose, it could open representative offices of the European Investment Bank (EIB) in the strategically chosen area and use the EIB as the financial arm to rally European companies under a consortia umbrella in order to bid effectively for projects in the area. They should acquire that knowledge which precedes wisdom by knowing what is going on in Southeast Asian markets. This implies: the creation of a competent, adequate and comprehensive intelligence/information gathering network, entreprenurially managed. It is essential to respond as rapidly as their competitors to challenges and opportunities. They should develop adequate systems for monitoring the policies of targeted Southeast Asian countries. The EU/national governments should assist targeted Southeast Asian markets in developing long-term measures to foster R&D capabilities of their industries.

## Adoption of a Continuous Learning Model

European companies must move from a state of unconscious ignorance to conscious competence. Links in the chain of acquiring knowledge about selected Southeast Asian countries must be established from ground level up and be aimed ultimately at establishing a network of offices in the region. This could be achieved with the support of the knowledge acquired by the many research centres on Asian Affairs scattered across the 15 states of the EU Members. This support can be mastered by pooling together their individual resources into a European–Asian databank which could be managed by a private business organization such as the European Federation of Industries. The European and Asian parties must both be willing to increase their knowledge of each other, for their mutual long-term benefit, through collaboration and co-operation, trust, commitment, perseverance, and adaptability, based on the understanding that they are stronger together than apart.

## Networking

A number of networking tools are available to European businesses looking to gain an understanding of the business climate in Southeast Asia and to forge business partnerships with Asian companies. For example, European Union representative offices, business information centres, antennas, etc. in Asia, chambers of commerce, industrial associations and trade organizations, as well as national embassies and consulates, are ready sources of information and introductions to potential clients or partners. (Possible disadvantages are the bureaucratic red tape involved in accessing information through this route.) In Europe, the Business Cooperation Network (BC-Net) is a computerized database developed by the European Union for the dissemination of information about Southeast Asia. Specialized trade journals and international newspapers (such as *The Far Eastern Economic Review, The Wall Street Journal Europe, Asia Inc, Asia Age, The Asian Wall Street Journal, The Economist, The International Herald Tribune*, and the *Financial Times*) provide up-to-date information on many aspects of doing business in Asia. Resourceful business people might tap into the European branches of the extensive networks of powerful and influential Asian families, such as those identified in *Asia Money* magazine in October–November 1994, as a way of facilitating later contacts in Asia. Business conferences on Southeast Asian affairs, especially those sponsored by Southeast Asian governments to attract foreign investors in their countries, are well set up for identifying investment opportunities and potential partners. The signing of letters of intent to become partners is a common outcome of such conferences. Other sources of information are specialist publications, such as the country reports produced by The Economist Intelligence Unit and studies produced by other international publishing companies.

Finally, one should not overlook one's personal ties and connections, and even the chance encounters one has on planes and at social functions, whether in Europe or in Asia.

## Developing an Awareness of Europe's Advantages over its Competitors

The bulk of European companies are small or medium-sized, as is also the case in Asia. Thus, Asian companies are likely to lack various resources that might be available through partnerships with similar-sized European companies. Their similar size also facilitates business relations, as there is a sense of equality between the partners that is lacking in ventures involving, say, a transnational or multinational company and a small or medium-sized Asian firm.

There are many similarities in the corporate or organizational cultures of technology-based medium-sized and small companies, regardless of their country of origin. Uppermost among these is their entrepreneurial spirit and relative lack of bureaucracy. The sharing of this spirit can foster a deeper understanding between the venture partners, whether they be French, German, Malaysian, or Filipino. This in turn makes the negotiating and collaboration process easier and more enriching.

Finally, there is the strength that comes from unity in diversity, which characterizes the economic policies of both the European and Southeast Asian nations. The cultural differences within Europe can be seen as a competitive advantage, a strength on which to build understanding with Asian cultures. Our cross-cultural experience as Europeans enables us to be aware of our own unique characteristics, as well as those of our European neighbours, to be flexible in the application of rules and values and able to reconcile differences, to support creativity, and to be wary of the influence of highly developed mass cultures. If Europe focuses on its own unique strengths, rather than on those of its competitors, it will be able to build successful partnerships with Asian companies who are aware of and in need of those particular attributes in a partner.

## HUMAN RESOURCE MANAGEMENT

### Selecting Suitable Expatriate Managers

As this book has made clear, the choice of who will be sent to manage a project in a Southeast Asian country will ultimately determine the effectiveness of the venture. In Asia, it must be remembered that the business context is only a small part of the whole philosophy of life, which is based on ideals of harmony, community, the avoidance of confrontation and a paternalistic relationship between employers and employees. The willingness or disposition of employees to commit themselves to the accomplishment of their tasks is determined by these variables. Therefore, a European manager who is not attuned to the prevailing philosophy and culture may fall wide of the mark in his or her dealings with local officials/staff.

Transforming a capable manager in Europe into a capable expatriate manager based in an Asian host country requires planning and the investment of resources. Planning encompasses analysis of the job content (responsibilities, tasks, activities, performance criteria, and so on), job context (working conditions such as deadlines and occupational hazards), reporting relationships, employee characteristics, and the interface between the organization and its external environment (government, competitors, and economic conditions).

## Hiring Local Personnel in the Host Country

The hiring of local managerial personnel in the host country is often best left to the local partner or to a personnel officer selected through the local branch of International Recruiting Firms (IRA). In some Southeast Asian countries, there may be a problem finding suitably qualified personnel. Indonesia has huge training needs, and Thailand's universities are not yet able to turn out enough engineering graduates to satisfy the industry demand. Freshly graduated engineers are also expensive in Thailand, commanding 15 000 baht (approximately US$96) per month in the first year and double that within two to three years. In the Philippines, on the other hand, there is an abundant supply of English-speaking college graduates (around one-third of the 800 000 or so Filipinos entering the work-force each year have university degrees), but they are more expensive than their Indonesian, Thai, and Vietnamese counterparts. This is not surprising, as Filipino senior and middle-level managers have an outstanding reputation in Southeast Asia. The main reason for their quality performance, apart from their professional training and experience, is the fact that the Philippines was colonized by Spain and then America, and was occupied by Japan during the Second World War. Thus, Filipinos have a flexible cultural outlook which is ideal for working in a cross-cultural environment.

## DEVELOPING AN ORGANIZATIONAL STRUCTURE

In this final part of the chapter we examine how the organizational structure of a company wishing to operate in Southeast Asia will be affected by its penetration strategy and adaptability to the targeted market(s). Organizational structure passes through five main phases.

### Phase 1: Learning by Listening to Potential Customers

During this phase, European headquarters begins its search for new business opportunities by gaining a preliminary understanding of the business climate in Southeast Asia and assessing the potential benefits of particular markets. The cultural issues and problems that are likely to be encountered in designing, planning, and implementing policies and strategies are identified in consultation with the various think tanks working on Asian affairs in Europe. Criteria are then developed for selecting representatives to visit the selected country or countries on an exploratory basis to test the results of their findings. During the visit, the representatives hold discussions with local and European officials, potential customers or partners, and other appropriate contacts identified during the preliminary research in Europe. On their return to Europe, they brief upper management on their findings about the needs of the targeted market(s) and begin to prepare detailed plans for a representative office which will transform the company's vision into a reality.

At this stage, suitable candidates to manage the company's representative office in the host country are identified and interviewed, together with their spouses. The successful candidate undergoes immersion training in the culture of the chosen country and the requirements of the job (see Chapter 8 for more detail on training) before leaving Europe to establish the company's representative office.

Once the manager is installed in Asia, regular visits are made to other countries in the region in order to develop a network of contacts among customers and suppliers. Regular (initially daily or weekly) reports are sent back to headquarters, which must in turn provide effective, timely support to the field office. A three-way relationship develops between the expatriate manager, local customers and suppliers, and European headquarters, with the representative manager acting as a cross-cultural communication "bridge" between the other two parties. Over time, the manager develops plans for expanding both actual and potential sales based on the feedback available from contacts cultivated in the region. This dedicated data network is crucial for growth, but is dependent upon the resident manager's and European headquarters' ability to learn by listening to local customers.

### Phase 2: Establishing a Regional Headquarters

As the company's business expands in the region, it becomes even more vital to maintain close contact with local customers through regular (ideally monthly) personal visits by the resident manager. The vast amount of travelling required of resident managers is essential for maintaining the friendships upon which business is based in Asia. However, this task may be so time-consuming that it leaves little time to attend to other essential matters, and it may become necessary to split the region between two resident managers with complementary areas of responsibility. The original manager's experience and contacts will be invaluable in staffing the second representative office and determining the two offices' responsibilities and geographical boundaries, and the form of collaboration between them. It is also important at this stage that European headquarters strengthens its support of the resident managers. It can do this by, for example, establishing marketing offices throughout the region to support the specialist work carried out by the regional managers through building up and strengthening the networks of customers and suppliers.

## Phase 3: Laying Down the Foundations for a Sound "Marriage"

Along with sales growth comes the realization that growth may not be sustainable for a number of reasons, including competitively priced local products and the fickleness of local consumers. At this stage, the momentum for autonomy from Europe starts gathering speed, which requires the laying of solid foundations for a sound "marriage" with the local markets. As a result of listening to and learning from their customers and suppliers, the resident representatives will be aware that if they are to continue to penetrate the local markets, they will have to change their strategic approach. For example, they may have to move from producing software to manufacturing hardware, or from selling products to sharing know-how. Rising fixed costs, and the production by local companies of cheaper versions of their products, necessitate being able to anticipate their customers' future requirements, rather than just servicing their present ones. Thus, it may be necessary to establish a manufacturing plant to meet those future needs.

The biggest barrier to implementing these strategic changes may come from European headquarters. It is up to the resident managers to convince upper management in Europe of the need to make the identified changes if the company is to continue to prosper in Southeast Asia, and to inspire them with their own vision of the possibilities inherent in the region. Once headquarters has agreed to support the proposed restructuring, it will be necessary for the resident managers to target a potential joint venture partner in the region. It is likely that this will be someone they have already done business with and with whom a solid friendship already exists. Negotiations will be carried out with the potential partner and local government officials to determine an acceptable package of investment incentives. Once negotiations are concluded and the agreements have been signed and approved, the newly established joint venture company is potentially ready to supply the domestic or regional market.

The process of becoming operational requires building the facilities, purchasing the required equipment, and hiring the necessary personnel. Although the back-up support of European headquarters is indispensable during this phase, it will be the resident managers, who have gained experience and knowledge on the ground, who will effect the transition process from courtship to "marriage".

### Phase 4: The "Wedding"

Once the resident representatives have implemented their strategic plan to increase their penetration of the Southeast Asian markets, the new plant will come into operation and the company will be open for business. During the first years, any organizational structure or staffing problems will be ironed out and business strategies will be continuously adapted to the ever-changing local conditions. A decision may be made to decentralize the company's operations, such as making the marketing companies more independent and transferring to them technical know-how and other resources and making them directly accountable to European headquarters. The regional offices may then be scaled down from co-ordinating the marketing units to managing agents throughout the region.

### Phase 5: "Married Life"

This final phase is the ultimate test of the joint venture's commitment to the growth of the Southeast Asian markets. It has been reached through a gradual, incremental, cumulative learning process. Throughout this phase, the joint venture will need to develop the ability to stay ahead of its competitors by innovating constantly, by being alert to changing tastes, and by continuously identifying and prioritizing potential markets in the region. It will be necessary to maximize the potential benefits deriving from the growth of markets in countries neighbouring the host country by identifying complementary resources and taking advantage of falling trade barriers. In short, its ability to expand its cross-border linkages will test its ability to open up new markets, develop old skills and acquire new ones, and create new technology and products by carrying out R&D

locally, while maintaining harmonious relations with the local partners in the spirit of their original agreement. This will be possible only if the European managers are familiar with and have fully adapted to the local culture. Diversification into neighbouring countries will require the same commitment to co-operative partnerships from the ground up.

## CONCLUSION

Joint ventures with foreign companies have been an appropriate means for many local companies in Southeast Asia to achieve growth and to expand into industrial conglomerates. Two such companies in Thailand are Saha Union and Siam Cement. Indeed, some European companies bypass some of the phases outlined above and go straight into joint venture agreements. The main focus of this chapter has been the need for European companies, whatever the form of their business associations in Southeast Asia, to learn how to change their attitudes and become skilled in operating in a cross-cultural context. Without effective cross-cultural communication, the links that make up the chain of customer/supplier networks will be flawed and prone to break down. As the forging of Europe Inc. is dependent on the efforts of individual companies, the future of Europe's role in the emerging markets of Southeast Asia will thus be threatened.

A bird's-eye view of joint venture fundamentals in developing and industrialized countries is presented in Appendix no. 17.

# 8
# Investing in Human Capital

## THE ASIAN "BRAIN BRIGADES"

Asian governments make unusually large investments in human capital. Extensive education and training programmes have been organized as part of a strategic approach aimed at strengthening the competitiveness of individual countries on the global economic stage. Part of the strategy is to draw on the educational resources offered in the West. The number of Asian students studying abroad, particularly in Western countries, has risen dramatically in the last decade. From 65 000 students in 1975, it has increased to half a million today. Each year, around 40 000 students come to Europe to study, while more than 200 000 take up further studies in North America. It is estimated that numbers will continue to grow at 10–15 per cent per annum. (By contrast, few European students study in Asia. For example, there are only half as many European students in Japan as American students.)

What are the reasons for this growth? The Asians see and perceive Europe with its humanistic culture and pessimistic attitude, as part of the past and America — with its technological culture and "can do" attitude — as the future. The Asian perception that an American education is more prestigious than a local one and will result in higher earnings is one factor. Europeans go to the United States for the very same reasons.

Another is the limited number of places in home country universities, combined with the aggressive recruitment drives by American universities. A further factor is the wide choice of courses offered by universities in the United States, although 60–75 per cent of Asians studying abroad take practical and career-oriented courses such as biochemistry, computer studies, engineering, medicine and mathematics. Australian higher education also has been particularly effective in marketing itself in Asia, notably in Southeast Asia. Australia probably takes as many students from ASEAN countries as the whole of the European Union, with only 5 per cent of the EU's population.

The strategy is paying high dividends. Singaporean, Malaysian, Indonesian, Thai, and other Asian students return from their studies in North America, Europe, and Australia with professional skills, knowledge of the West, vital contacts, and an attachment to their Alma Mater universities. They return to Asia for a variety of reasons: good job offers, the desire to be part of their country's rapid growth, and entrepreneurial aspirations. Five years after completing their studies, most students will hold key positions in government or local industry, or will be running their own businesses.

Students attending overseas schools have considerable buying power in their host country. As they come from elite families, they are able to afford the high tuition fees, and tend to spend freely during their time abroad. Thus, an overseas education generates short-term benefits for the host country, as well as long-term benefits for the home country.

Asian students based in North America, Europe, and Australia are exposed to the cultural traditions of those countries. This cultural immersion can prove invaluable in their later commercial dealings with Westerners. In this they have a decided advantage over Western students who tend to have little knowledge of the socio-economic developments taking place in Asia today.

## THE NEED FOR ACADEMIC CO-OPERATION AND MANAGEMENT TRAINING PROGRAMMES

A number of innovative programmes for the promotion of academic co-operation with Asia have been introduced in EU countries in recent years. For example, the Academic Cooperation Association (ACA) is an independent European organization dedicated to the support, improvement, management, and analysis of academic co-operation within Europe and between Europe and the rest of the world. It was created in July 1993 with the legal status of a non-profit-making international association according to Belgian law. The members of the ACA, which is based in Brussels, are major agencies located in European Union and European Free Trade Association (EFTA) countries responsible for the promotion of international academic co-operation.

Some professionals recommend a strategy which would go beyond merely improving the marketing of European higher education in Asia, although boosting the flow of students from Asia would certainly be attractive to many EU countries. The view is that the European Union should focus on developing programmes targeting specific groups in order to enhance co-operation with and competitiveness in Asia, through the development of appropriate human resources, both Asian and European.

The need for such programmes is mounting, given the declining European presence in Asia's booming business markets. One reason for this has been the high costs of sending European business people on overseas assignments. It costs most companies between three and five times an employee's basic salary to maintain the employee and his or her family in a foreign posting. This has resulted in an increasing trend to hire host or third-country nationals to fill top positions. The increasing influence of Japan in the Southeast Asian markets is also apparent. Some 90 000 Japanese professionals work in countries in Southeast Asia, and in the process are extending Japan's impact on management practices in the region. Countries such as Singapore are seeking not only to attract their own nationals studying abroad, but also scientists, engineers, and managers from other Asian countries who have been trained abroad. Around 6000 Japanese are employed in Singapore. This trend seems to indicate that some Asian countries are looking to create a regional R&D environment to offset the apparent inability of Westerners to adapt to an Asian environment.

This mix of foreign professionals reflects a new policy integration trend, as described in the UN *World Investment Report 1993*:

> "For TNCs [transnational companies], investment, trade, technology transfer and the movement of staff are often interrelated ways of expanding abroad. In fact, integrated production strategies typically required that each of these channels is open to a firm, depending on its needs and the nature of a market. Accordingly, a rounded and outward-oriented development strategy is indispensable if a country wants to become part of the emerging system of international production. But more is required. In the same manner in which TNCs consider FDI [foreign direct investment], trade, technology transfer and the movement of technical personnel as interrelated, so too must governments consider their policies in these areas as interrelated. In other words, governments must reexamine each policy proposal for its impact on the other policy areas and its implications for the wider strategy."[1]

At the bottom line for any company doing business overseas, and in Southeast Asia in particular, is total quality performance. Managers' performance is dependent upon their fully understanding the environment in which they operate. In a cross-cultural environment, the difficulties of correctly interpreting one's environment and colleagues are compounded by differences in language, and cultural values and expectations.

Cross-cultural researchers have identified three types of cultural interpretation:

1. *Subconscious cultural blunders*—the tendency to make subconscious, culturally-based assumptions about events, people and behaviour.
2. *Lack of cultural awareness*—a lack of awareness of our own cultural characteristics. That is, our inability to see ourselves as others see us, and our lack of understanding of how our

own culture has influenced our behaviour and decision-making process.
3. *Projected similarities and parochialism*—our tendency to assume that people and situations in other cultures are similar to our own.

A further area of concern is the self-reliance criterion (SRC). SRC is the unconscious tendency to refer to one's own cultural values when evaluating situations in other cultural environments. Some researchers considered this form of cultural interpretation as the cause of most international business problems and suggested a four-step approach in identifying SRC and minimizing the resulting errors in judgement:

1. Define the business problem or goal in terms of your own cultural traits, habits, and norms.
2. Define the same problem or goal in terms of the foreign cultural traits, habits, and norms, without making a value judgement.
3. Isolate the influence of SRC and examine how it complicates the problem or goal.
4. Redefine the problem or goal without the influence of SRC and solve for the optimum business situation.

In an article entitled "Multicultural Perspectives on European and Asian Management",[2] Professors Georges Hirsch (former Director of the European School of Management, Paris (EAP)) and Frederick Swierczek (of the Asian Institute of Technology in Bangkok) explored the effects of multiculture on management and organizations. They concluded that a European style of management would emerge from greater integration of the European Union and would be characterized by sensitivity to the values associated with that integration. Good management, they believed, is always in some sense transcultural; that is, management practices may have their roots in different cultural milieu, but in practice the best approaches are adopted because they work, not because they fit a set of cultural assumptions. They are transcultural because they move beyond the limits of national cultures. In terms of a convergence of management styles, Hirsch and Swierczek concluded that the essence of the approach is to recognize which features of management and organization translate well across cultures; to be sensitive to how culture influences management processes between people of different backgrounds; to develop a multicultural organizational strategy through a team-orientation; and to aim towards creating an organization which is transcultural because it has created its own shared vision and values beyond the individual national cultures it represents.

For managers operating across national boundaries and with subordinates with different cultural and professional identities, developing an awareness of how to work together is essential. In the future, creating an appropriate organizational or corporate culture may be the most important task in achieving success as a multicultural organization. Thus, investment in human capital—in training the next generation of managers in how to achieve results in a multicultural world—is an all-important step in creating Europe Inc.

## THE CHARACTERISTICS AND CONTENT OF PROPOSED MANAGEMENT TRAINING PROGRAMMES

The new discipline of cross-cultural research is a direct result of the internationalization of business. As already stated, this comparative research focuses on the similarities and differences between organizations in diverse institutions and societies as ultimate products of their cultural milieus. Some researchers have argued that the research carried out in the West (very little has been done on Southeast Asian countries) is aimed at learning from the new industrial leaders, especially Japan, and that its focus is the relationship between the state and other interest groups rather than the internal dynamics of organizations. Others argue that the research reveals differences between organizations in different cultures which are relevant to programmes aimed at teaching managers how to negotiate and operate effectively in a cross-cultural context.

Management training programmes might include those designed for senior European executives who will be participating in negotiations to establish a joint venture in a Southeast Asian country, as well as those aimed at European personnel who have been selected for a long-term posting in Asia. The programmes should be designed to increase awareness of other cultures in general, and the selected host country in particular. Would-be expatriates need to be made aware of the implications of working in Southeast Asia and be helped to overcome the tendency to make judgements based on their own culture.

Programmes should be designed and implemented by both seasoned European and Asian professionals. Without an in-depth understanding of what is happening in a particular Southeast Asian economy and society, a European joint venture partner will have little chance of completing the venture successfully and, by extension, creating a positive impression of Europe in Asia.

Programmes should have clearly defined goals in terms of cross-cultural communication and performance, based on the transfer and development of new knowledge from which new skills can be developed. They should be designed and implemented by managers who are successfully operating in Southeast Asia, by professional management experts (such as affiliates of the European Institute for Advanced Studies in Management), or by Southeast Asian professionals (such as those attached to the Asian Institute of Technology in Bangkok or at the Institute of Technology, Bandung, Indonesia) or government officials. All such programmes should be managed and co-ordinated by one organization, preferably one in the private sector (such as Bocconi University in Milan or a similar institution) with the appropriate sponsorship.

Programmes should include courses on such subjects as:

- *Overcoming cultural bias*—that is, developing an awareness of one's own cultural system by interacting with others who do not share that system. Special attention should be given to comparative cognitive processes. The discussion leader should prepare appropriate background material.

- *Cultural sensitivity*—that is, learning how to exercise cultural sensitivity in social interaction with Asian business people and government officials with different linguistic and cultural backgrounds.
- *Language*—that is, acquiring some proficiency in the main language spoken in the target country.
- *Company growth*—that is, the process of moving from a domestic to a global orientation.
- *Host country government*—that is, the relationship between the host country's government and local firms. This illustrates how a particular government can influence business negotiations and the consequent appropriate patterns of behaviour when dealing with government officials.
- *Host country cultural values*—that is, the key values, attitudes, and customs in the host country. This enables the European manager to understand local attitudes towards time-keeping, work, achievement, wealth and material gain, change and/or risk perception, transfer of technology, and human development.
- *Global economy*—that is, how it works and the role of the Southeast Asian economies, especially in relation to foreign direct investment.
- *European Union–ASEAN relations*—that is, the present status of institutionalized development within the WTO frame of reference and its impact on company operations overseas.
- *National stereotyping*—that is, how the trainees' national culture perceives the nationals of the host country, and how the citizens of individual Southeast Asian countries view Europeans. Both views are essential in order to stress the importance of the stereotype in providing a reference point.
- *Transnational companies–host country relations*—that is, the relations between any transnational company and a host country should be considered in the historical context of relations between transnational companies and developing countries. Comprehensive use could be made of the databases of the OECD, the United Nations Center for Multinational Companies (UNCMC), the World Bank, and EU institutions.
- *Comparative management styles*—that is, a comparison between the management cultures of the European and host countries.

Information is available from a variety of sources, although there is very little available on the managerial style of European managers in Southeast Asia.

- *Negotiations*—that is, case studies of successes and failures in negotiations between EU officials/companies and local Asian firms.
- *Managing joint ventures*—that is, the planning, setting up, developing, and management of joint ventures.
- *Foreign direct investment flows*—that is, how foreign direct investment anticipates and follows trade between developing and developed countries.
- *Foreign direct investment regulation*—that is, the foreign direct investment regimes in different countries, and studies by the International Monetary Fund.

## CONCLUSION

In this chapter we examined the implications of investing in human capital, stressed the strategic need for training programmes for European would-be expatriate managers in Southeast Asia, and made recommendations as to the content of such programmes. The chapter concludes our discussion in Part III of what European companies, both transnational and small to medium-sized, can do in helping to create Europe Inc. in the emerging markets of Southeast Asia. The final part of this book offers some global conclusions.

## ENDNOTES

[1]UN *World Investment Report 1993*, p. 224.

[2]Hirsch, Georges and Swierczek, Frederick (1993) "Multicultural Perspectives on European and Asian Management", *European Management Journal* (20th Anniversary Issue), pp. 17–27.

# Part IV
## GLOBAL CONCLUSIONS

# 9
# Global Conclusions

This book has examined the fundamental question of why European companies do not have a stronger and more assertive presence in Asia in general, and in the emerging markets of Southeast Asia in particular. Forming successful joint ventures with Asian partners requires a daunting amount of strategic planning organization/financial engineering, flexibility in services, co-ordination, support, political clout, cross-cultural teamwork and a commitment by both parties to their shared vision and a consensus form of decision-making over the long term.

The advantages of joint ventures include better market access, lower manufacturing costs, technological improvements, and economies of scale in product development and production. These advantages provide the incentive to overcome differences between the parties' ethnicities, cultural values, and business practices. However, in the long term, continued co-operation will be dependent upon their abilities to communicate cross-culturally, and to incorporate ongoing learning and flexibility into their relationship. The joint venture must be able to adapt to changes in their own individual and mutual needs and those of the market-place. Difficulties may arise as the joint venture matures if there was insufficient or inadequate pre-planning in terms of the practical functioning of the operation, if the parties failed to take the time to fully understand each other and to negotiate consensus decisions, and if there has been a lack of policy agreement on matters such as dividend policies, capital increases, investment plans, transfer pricing, and so on.

The success of the joint venture will be contingent upon both parties' willingness and determination to meet the needs of the venture during both the planning and operation stages. This agreement implies that both partners give priority to the welfare of the venture. Like a marriage, a joint venture is not self-perpetuating and self-sufficient, but must be consciously maintained through involvement and commitment. The bottom line is co-operation, where decision-making is shared between them, not perpetual negotiation. And at the root of co-operation is sound cross-cultural communication.

The ultimate result of any business venture is success or failure. Thus, embarking on a venture is both a risk and an opportunity. In Southeast Asia, a European partner's willingness to take calculated and imaginative risks, and to see them as opportunities in the long run, is perceived by the Asian partner as an indication of acceptance of the Asian philosophy of life and a willingness to work within that context, as well as of the entrepreneurial ability that is necessary for performing in a cross-cultural milieu. Dr Supachai Panipchpakdi, former Deputy Prime Minister of Thailand, expressed a view widely shared throughout Southeast Asia when he said in an interview with the *Europa Times* in October 1994:

> "We have noticed that those companies who have invested in Asia are now more profitable than those companies who have not. The Europeans are less enterprising than the Japanese and the Taiwanese, and more cautious."[1]

There is nothing miraculous about the Asian "miracle" economies. Two decades ago, Asia was at a crossroads, its strategic direction in doubt due to Marxist insurgencies and the fear in the West of the spread of communism throughout the region, as expressed in the domino theory. The miracle that is evident in Southeast Asia today has come about through sheer hard work, coupled with low taxes, high saving rates, minimal government intervention, and access to export credits. Asian business people have an unusual capacity for taking a pragmatic approach, plus the will to experiment, learn, adjust, and persevere under difficult circumstances. The longevity of Asian governments has meant that what government intervention *has* occurred has taken place in a disciplined and co-ordinated manner. There has been an exceptionally large investment in and efficient use of both physical and human capital, such as the development of scarce management resources and entrepreneurial capacity. While the leaders of the High-Performance Asian Economies (HPAEs) have tended to be either authoritarian or paternalistic, they have also been willing to grant genuine authority to technocratic elites and to key leaders of the private sector. Unlike authoritarian leaders in many other economies, leaders in the HPAEs have realized that economic development requires co-operation. The emerging Southeast Asian economies have also demonstrated a greater thirst for knowledge about Europe and Western business practices than Europeans have shown to date about Asia.

While a sense of regional community has emerged unguided in Southeast Asia in recent years, the 15 nations comprising the European Union are still struggling to forge a unity that will determine its role in the global economy and transcultural world of the 21st century. It is hoped that this book has shown the way forward for European companies, both transnational and small to medium-sized, who are willing to overcome cultural barriers both home and abroad in order to forge a dynamic and innovative Europe Inc. able to take its rightful place alongside USA Inc., Japan Inc., and the emerging markets of Southeast Asia on the global economic stage.

## ENDNOTE

[1]From *Europa Times*, October 1994, p. 4. Reproduced by permission.

# Appendix No. 1
# The Importance of Southeast Asia to Europe
# A Simplified Quantified Approach

| Country | Population (m) 1995 | GDP Growth Rates, Percentage Per Annum | | | | | | | | |
|---|---|---|---|---|---|---|---|---|---|---|
| | | 1989 | 1990 | 1991 | 1992 | 1993 | 1994 | 1995 | 1996* | 1997* |
| Brunei | 0.292 | 1.0 | 1.0 | 1.1 | 1.3 | 1.6 | n.a. | n.a. | n.a. | n.a. |
| Indonesia | 196.7 | 7.5 | 7.2 | 7.0 | 6.5 | 6.5 | 7.5 | 7.6 | 7.3 | 7.3 |
| Malaysia | 19.9 | 9.2 | 9.7 | 8.7 | 7.8 | 8.3 | 8.7 | 8.5 | 8.5 | 8.0 |
| Philippines | 68.6 | 6.2 | 3.0 | −0.6 | 0.3 | 2.1 | 4.3 | 5.0 | 5.5 | 6.5 |
| Singapore | 2.93 | 9.2 | 8.8 | 6.7 | 6.0 | 10.1 | 10.1 | 9.0 | 8.5 | 8.5 |
| Thailand | 59.5 | 12.2 | 11.6 | 8.4 | 7.9 | 8.2 | 8.5 | 8.7 | 8.4 | 8.0 |
| Vietnam | 72.5 | 7.8 | 5.0 | 6.0 | 8.7 | 8.1 | 8.8 | 9.6 | 9.8 | 8.0 |

Source: Asian Development Bank/World Bank
*Estimates

# Appendix No. 2
# Lessons to be Drawn from World Experiences

| World | Europe | Asia |
|---|---|---|
| From the globalization/regionalization experience, the following lessons can be drawn. These two complementary realities are based upon:<br>• maximizing *information*;<br>• developing an *awareness* of what is actually going on;<br>• *changing of attitudes*; and ultimately, behaviour;<br>• *developing* sound and consistent *policies* aimed at opening the EU market to the developing world and making proper assessment of the impact of these policies on the developing countries;<br>• *internationalizing attitudes* by:<br>– engaging in more balanced and sustainable economic policies;<br>– acting on opportunities, not viewing them as threats, and<br>– speed of action; | From Europe's cultural dynamics, the following experiences can be highlighted:<br>• European cultural diversity is seen:<br>– *as a strength* by those with an international attitude in the global market-place while carving out Europe's role in the world, and<br>– *as a weakness* by those who have not yet developed this international attitude; they are concerned only with preserving the cultural matrix they were born in without perceiving its position within a European context;<br>• *cultural diversity* in Europe is a force of solidarity and social cohesiveness;<br>• *European cultures* are not threatened by the idea of a united Europe able to speak with one voice on the world stage; | From an analysis of the Asian miracles, the following lessons can be drawn:<br>• *Miracles are not impossible, because they are the result of:*<br>– development strategies carefully matched to a country's institutional capacity and economic environment, and<br>– the adaptation of policies, experimentation, and pragmatic reforms, not the result of luck<br>• *Repeating the Asian miracles* depends on how one views these successes. If they are attributed to the Asians' outward attitude, one may be optimistic; if they are attributed to deeper cultural and institutional causes, less so. The truth perhaps lies midway.<br>• *Major factors in these miracles were*:<br>– savings,<br>– the need for them, |

| World | Europe | Asia |
|---|---|---|
| • *increasing global competition in European markets;*<br>• *creating strategic business intelligence networks* and continuously monitoring their effectiveness;<br>• *contributing with cross-cultural ideas* and concepts to negotiations; and<br>• *carving out the role of the private sector* by regulatory efficiency rather than deregulation. | • *European managers* have learnt at home how to do business in a multicultural environment;<br>• *cultural alertness* helps people to successfully manage brand portfolios in global markets; and<br>• if Europe does *not* try *to imitate* its competitors, but maximizes its own strengths, it will also succeed in partnerships with the developing world. | – unusual capacity for pragmatic government,<br>– experimentation,<br>– learning,<br>– capacity to adjust to changing circumstances,<br>– longevity of governments,<br>– administrative set-up, and<br>– exceptional large investments in human and physical capital.<br>• *What has changed* is: strategies that rely on import technology.<br>• *What has not changed* is: the attraction of East Asia as a production location. |

# Appendix No. 3 The 5Ws of the Global Communication Process and Cross-Cultural Communication Issues and Problems

| No. | Question | Cross-cultural dynamics |
|---|---|---|
| 1 | What is culture? | – Endless definitions throughout the course of history<br>– It is an extremely broad concept<br>– In a sense there is no "true" culture *per se* for the meaning of culture varies according to who is reporting/ experiencing it (what, whom, where, when, why and with whom)<br>– Essentially a collective concept absorbed by individuals with varying degrees of accuracy and intensity which has the effect of modifying culture itself<br>– There are different levels of cultures<br>– For the purpose of this study we refer only to:<br>• cultures in Southeast Asia (SEA)<br>• cultures in European countries<br>• corporate cultures of transnational corporations (TCs) (Europe) operating in SEA. |
| 2 | Why is culture important? | – Because to operate a business venture in SEA it is vital for a European working for a TC to interact on a daily basis over the long term with all the citizens of the host country in which he is living and working<br>– The success of these European expatriates will depend upon the successful outcome of this interaction<br>– It conditions most of our actions and feelings and therefore also those of expatriate managers and executives<br>– It is not innate but learned<br>– Large portions of our decisions are determined by culture. |
| 3 | What are the dimensions of culture and cross-cultures? | – Attitudes, behaviour, values, beliefs which the European TC holds in and how they affect:<br>• what these expatriates are trying to do with their host country partners and with their executives in their home (European) country<br>• who has power, authority, responsibility etc. while operating their business ventures in host country<br>• how their different roles will be played |

| No. | Question | Cross-cultural dynamics |
|---|---|---|
| | | • where rewards for their work are granted<br>• when "sanctions" are going to be applied<br>• what aspects of European and Asian culture should be adapted in order to share decision-making processes with the host country partner. |
| 4 | Who interacts with whom? | – those providing the resources (i.e. labour, time and effort, financial capital, natural resources and other material inputs to the JV) that the TC must acquire in order to:<br>• produce its products/services<br>• satisfy the consumers/market for those products/services<br>• comply with/adapt requests and suggestions from government agencies<br>– Communicating information and ideas<br>– Negotiating |
| 5 | How do they interact? | – Buying<br>– Selling<br>– Delivering products and/or services<br>– Receiving payments<br>– Responding to data, technological know-how, managerial directives, etc. received in writing or verbally. Thus, increasing<br>– Potential for understanding/misunderstandings<br>– Using a high level of cultural/cross-cultural awareness and empathy (especially on the part of the European expatriates) whose interaction is based on their<br>– Ability to adjust to the cultural milieu without living in expatriate "ghettos"<br>– Transcending the boundaries of their own separate cultures<br>– Transferring resources (TC) including people and products between TC headquarters in Europe and host country<br>– Recognizing cultural differences and appropriately decoding/interpreting them and their implications for headquarters. |
| 6 | Where do they interact? | – Within the resources/product market and political and legal systems which are<br>– Products of the prevailing host country culture<br>– In ways that are dictated by the accepted norms and values of that culture. |
| 7 | When is this interaction important? | – When forming harmonious relations with Asian citizens<br>– When adjustment to cultural differences is required because it might affect the long-term profitability/health of the JV<br>– Whenever cultural sensitivity may *also* be translated into sound business policies and practices. |
| 8 | How to respond when cross-cultural problems arise? | – Increase use of host country nationals in the design and implementation of business ventures for their country<br>– Decentralize managerial responsibilities<br>– Generate benefits by effectively using overseas professional abilities in a consulting capacity<br>– Organize training programmes for host country HR |

(*Continued*)

| No. | Question | Cross-cultural dynamics |
|---|---|---|
| | | – Design, develop and implement culturally oriented training programmes for European TC personnel before their arrival in host country, and their families |
| 9 | What is the impact of a European TC on local culture(s)? | – Knowledge and skills<br>• The role TCs play in spreading knowledge and skills is much more than "technology transfer"<br>• TC's manpower development in the host country is an investment. They capitalize on training costs in the same fashion as on plants and machinery. This varies among TCs according to:<br>• the sector<br>• the level of industrialization of the country<br>• the capital or labour utilized<br>• respective corporate personnel and policies<br>• the intensive nature of the technology used<br>• From the host country viewpoint what is essential is not just the skills created within the confines of the local JV but also their desire for a European TC presence which is likely to engineer a cascade of benefits involving not only the people working directly with the TC but the nation as a whole (also because of increased exports) together with the other sectors of the national economy<br>• TC news agencies. Since the beginning of the 20th century 4–5 news services have dominated the world supply in international and national news for the written and visual media and government agencies. They are controlled by DdCs but they have made people in SEA aware of events in the rest of the world and vice versa. They have formed the world's image of SEA countries by reporting their news<br>• US–UK based news services have spread English as a truly international language including in SEA<br>• TC book publishing. Publishers are increasingly extending their operations to SEA to include:<br>• scientific, technical and general books<br>• local authors<br>• reprints from home countries<br>They are extending their operations because of the labour cost advantage in producing cheap editions affordable to host country students and public/libraries<br>– Cultural identity. TCs facilitate the movement of:<br>• factors of production and products across national borders together with their underlying ideas, philosophies, values and behavioural patterns<br>• business culture(s)<br>• transnational spread of music, the arts, literature and films from Europe to SEA countries and vice versa, but also to the rest of the world |

| No. | Question | Cross-cultural dynamics |
|---|---|---|
| | | • consumer patterns and the consumer society<br>They also create attitudes of cultural ambivalence in the elite. People begin to question the lifestyle, beliefs, value system, world view and the arts of both Europe and SEA, developing a feeling of inferiority/superiority about their own cultural systems. This ambivalent attitude may revolve around the following issues:<br>• They want the TC to be a transmitter of<br>• capital<br>• technology<br>• "modern" values<br>• behavioural patterns<br>There is a belief that these are the reasons for the prosperity of the developed world and want the same for their countries<br>• They are uncomfortable with this very dependence. Thus they:<br>• resent being manipulated by outside organizations<br>• become aware of their own limitations when TCs move in. |

## Global Communication Process and Cross-Cultural Communications Issues and problems

| No. | Question | Global communication process |
|---|---|---|
| 1 | Why is communication important? | – The purpose of communicating is to promote something<br>– The purpose of promoting is to inform, educate, persuade or stimulate an appropriate response from a particular market or market segment<br>– It is essentially the same for both national and global markets<br>– The process cannot be left to chance. |
| 2 | What is communication? | – A promotional strategy which blends four areas into one: advertising, publicity, sales promotion and self-assertion. |
| 3 | How is the communication process structured in the marketplace? | – Five elements interact:<br>• a sender<br>• a receiver (audience)<br>• a message<br>• a communication channel<br>• feedback. |
| 4 | What are the attributes of effective communication? | – A clear understanding of the message by the communicator<br>– The communicator must know the audience and its composition<br>– He must understand how his audience will interpret and respond to the message |

(*Continued*)

| No. | Question | Global communication process |
|---|---|---|
| | | – Use of socio-cultural clues and symbols familiar to the receiver (to ensure the message is acted upon by the receiver)<br>– A medium that is socio-culturally and legally appropriate. |
| 5 | Where are the barriers to effective communication? | – Discrepancies between the home market and foreign market<br>– Differences in socio-cultural and economic factors giving rise to different perceptions of buyer's behaviour and of product<br>– Difference in languages:<br>• need to go well beyond a literal translation of the message<br>• language suffers in translation<br>• the spirit of the local language has to be taken into account<br>• what is effective in one language may mean something very offensive in another or be ludicrous<br>• the original message has to be put into the local languages to mirror local culture, to convey the real meaning of the message<br>• changes have to be fundamentally made in: brandnames, sales promotion material and advertising when used locally in slogans<br>– Cultural differences. When a TC in a JV with a local firm decides to launch an awareness campaign to improve its chances of penetrating the local market it uses an advertising strategy. But sometimes ads adversely affect the market, due to values, colour preferences, gestures etc. In Indonesia many companies overcome this problem using the Wayang Kulit story (puppet show)<br>– Social differences. Differing attitudes among consumers towards advertising may be rooted in historical and social bias. The concern voiced in one country is not necessarily valid in another. Given the multi-ethnic societies of SEA this potential communication barrier may be even more powerful<br>– Economic differences, including:<br>• degree of urbanization<br>• households may have radios but not tv sets<br>• markets are widely dispersed, as in the case of the Philippines and Indonesia formed by many islands<br>• written communication is not as effective as visual or oral communication because of local traditions and/or literacy skills, as in the case of the Philippines where demonstration shows or cars with loudspeakers are frequently used<br>• discretionary incomes of individuals and families directly affect their attitudes towards products. For example in Sulawesi, the purchasing power is 40 per cent that of cosmopolitan Jakarta<br>• necessities in one country are luxuries in another |

| No. | Question | Global communication process |
|---|---|---|
| | | – Legal and regulatory differences<br>Local advertising regulations and industrial codes vary dramatically throughout SEA. Yet they directly influence the media and the content of promotional materials<br>– Competitive differences. The nature of regional, national or global competiton has a significant impact on communication. In fact, expenditure on communication, its frequency, its approach and channels are determined by:<br>• intensity of competition<br>• the rate at which product innovation is introduced<br>• national, regional, global communication strategies<br>• competitors' reactions. |
| 6 | How to communicate a response to a political risk? | – Making periodic assessments of the political climate in the region/country on the basis of which decisions will also be made on:<br>• whether to invest or not in any given country of SEA<br>• which type of business operation is considered to be (by both TC and host country) the most appropriate<br>• whether to expand, continue or reduce presence in host country<br>– More widely used methods of responding to political risks are:<br>• JVs<br>• other agreements, that is, developing linkages with local suppliers, distributors or dependent industries<br>• pre-arranged disinvestment or domestication<br>• strong home country support. |

# Appendix No. 4
# Comparing European and Asian Management Styles

BASIC VALUES

| *European* | *Asian* |
|---|---|
| Judeo-Christian | Buddhist-Confucian |
| Human beings are fundamentally bad | Human beings are potentially good |
| Legalistic constraints and supporting institutions | Social and community constraints |
| Concentrates on legitimacy in a confrontation | Concentrates on compromise, trust and confidence in others |
| Pre-eminence of individual | Pre-eminence of group |
| Analytic orientation (Cartesian) | Fluent approach — handles ambiguity |
| – precise | – imprecise |
| – explicit | – implicit |

ORGANIZATIONAL DIMENSIONS

| *European* | *Asian* |
|---|---|
| Co-ordination formal | Co-ordination informal |
| – functional | – relationship |
| – organigram | – multiple roles |
| – delegation | – action based on expectations |
| Organization fragmented by specialization | Organization very integrated |
| Contract directed | Agreement — understood |
| Hierarchical model | Family model |
| Individual decision-making | Collective decision-making |
| – one right decision | – compromise |
| – constrained by competition and confrontation | – based on co-operative solution of harmony |

MANAGEMENT PHILOSOPHIES

| *European* | *Asian* |
|---|---|
| Emphasizes debate and rationality | Emphasizes relationship within the group |
| External concerns | Internal concerns |
| Economic/utility focus | Social focus |
| Structured | Flexible |
| Quantitative — number oriented | Qualitative/appropriateness |
| Change by imposition and force | Change by natural process — continuous and adjusting |

MANAGEMENT PHILOSOPHIES

| | |
|---|---|
| Legitimation by techno-structure | Legitimated by social equilibrium |
| Importance of basic principles | Importance of form and context |
| Metaphor: to do, to know | Metaphor: to be, to understand |

MANAGERIAL FEATURES

| *European* | *Asian* |
|---|---|
| **Management Perspective** | |
| Results — short term | Market share<br>Long-range profit |
| Management by control | Strategic management<br>Human resources |
| Rational organization | Informal/temporary organization |
| Bureaucratic | Concentrating on activities |
| Division of labour | |
| Limited range of opportunities | |
| Restricted by specific competence | |
| Human resource perspective | Human resource perspective |
| – cost | – performance and quality |
| – control | – positive expectations |
| – negative expectations | – employee priority |
| – industrial conflict | – continuous improvement |
| – problem solving | – emphasizes agreement |
| – conflict resolution | |
| One-way marketing | Two-way marketing oriented to customer demand |
| **Leadership style** | |
| Overt — Directive | Subtle — Indirect, collaborating |
| Decision-making affirmed by action of subordinate | Decision affirmed by agreement or implementing subordinates |
| Manager dominates | Balance of interests |
| Emotional involvement of decision-maker | Mutual involvement of subordinates |

Source: *European Management Journal*, 20th anniversary issue, 1993.

# Appendix No. 5 Outline of Cross-Cultural Characteristics: Europe vs Southeast Asia (SEA)—A Brush Stroke Approach

| No | Similarities | No | Differences |
|---|---|---|---|
| 1 | Any kind of intervention in the management field inevitably supports the interests of those who are already in power, whether they be the elite within a country or business, or the elite nations of the world (i.e. foreign aid given for the ultimate benefit of donors). | 1 | Style:<br>– SEA: largely Muslim/Buddhist cultures stressing traditional social relations and obligations<br>– Europe: largely Christian, predominantly capitalist cultures, stressing competition and individualism. |
| 2 | Purchasing power between white-collar workers, high-income earners, higher education, luxury products consumers, youth products (jeans, music . . .), low-price high value products, i.e. Benetton etc. | 2 | Resources and infrastructure: taken for granted in Europe while they do not exist to the same extent or not at all in some parts of the countries in SEA. |
| | | 3 | Communication and energy are much less reliable in SEA than in Europe. |
| | | 4 | Homogeneous, SEA vs heterogeneous European family groups. It takes a homogeneous group to preserve cultural values. With the present decline of family traditions in Europe and more single |

3 European companies wish to move to SEA because of the advantages of a large market interested in receiving more European business ventures. SEA wishes to initiate business in Europe for the very same reason. This interest is coupled with the comparatively greater risks of doing business overseas.

4 Purchasing power among nations within Europe.

5 The process which binds together blocks of countries (i.e. Europe/SEA/ASEAN), organizations, groups and even individuals is essentially perceived as a continuous exchange of both material and non-material commodities.

6 The importance of communication is widely and evenly stressed throughout the EC and ASEAN countries. At the same time complaints are constantly being aired about poor communication even within the same business organization (be it in KL or Berlin, in Jakarta or in Rome).

7 Travel arrangement (mostly by plane).

8 Time zones within European countries and within SEA countries.

9 Linguistic differences between Europe and SEA are being minimized because of the spread of a neutral language: English.

10 Knowledge needed to mobilize resources and to produce commodities. Knowledge, as a commodity itself, creates innovation as it is transferred all over the world.

11 Management and leadership: *what* to lead, i.e. what is needed.

12 Organization of production and patterns of work are the result of aspirations for similar kinds of organizational goals. As the industrialization process continues, the production technology and its corresponding machinery tend to become more and people in society, cross-cultural barriers are rapidly dissolving within Europe (thanks also to TV and low airfares allowing young generations to travel and receive exposure to cultures).

5 The balance of power within a marriage is being influenced by the interaction of comparative resources such as education, income and occupational status of husband and wife and cultural expectations about who does what.

6 Consumer tastes, habits and income vary.

7 Materialistic consumption societies of Europe vs. SEA countries where the "comfort" approach is just beginning to spread.

8 Geographical distances.

9 Time zones between Europe and SEA.

10 Linguistic differences between Europe and SEA very strong for people over 50.

11 Barriers preventing one from doing things, i.e. reading publications etc. especially comparing Europe to SEA.

12 Conceptual barriers.

13 Management and leadership: *how* to lead, especially in human resources.

14 Concept of time: Europe linear, SEA circular.

15 Patterns of living, the existence and use of time, both lifetime and weekly/daily time—a major difference between Europe and SEA.

16 Wage differentials between Europe and SEA up to the white collar workers.

(*Continued*)

| No | Similarities | No | Differences |
|---|---|---|---|
| | more similar and the problems and solutions concerning the organization of production as well as people also begin to move closer to each other. | 17 | Economic structure, i.e. the mechanism for regulating and guiding the use of scarce resources (natural, means of production, labour etc.) provided by the environment. |
| 13 | Patterns of living within Europe. | 18 | Political structure which includes method of selecting state leadership, mechanisms for developing public policy, means for administering the state operations and the system of law. |
| 14 | Decisions concerning one's wages are less and less made through the influence of an individual worker or even an enterprise. Economic rewards are decided outside the organization where the individual works. | 19 | Value structure, instrumental values which indicate how different instruments and means are used to reach the goal. |
| 15 | Real relation of economic rewards to work behaviour and satisfaction. | 20 | Ways of accomplishing the manager's goal vary between Europe and SEA and within Europe and SEA. Example: in Malaysia, Indonesia, Thailand, it would be seen as considerate to discuss a subordinate's personal difficulties in their absence, because it would express local cultures where it is more tactful if a personal difficulty can be resolved without discussion and in public. In sharp contrast this is found to be highly inconsiderate in Europe. |
| 16 | Common environmental threats: air and water pollution and terrorism, so far limited to hijacking but in the case of chemical, nuclear threats then co-operation must also overcome ideological barriers. | 21 | Singing organization's songs and regular socializing after hours. |
| 17 | Distribution and significance of economic rewards have come to be increasingly based on merit and seniority rather than an inherited status or political acceptability. | 22 | Europe/SEA markets differ in their language and method of communication, beliefs and attitudes, values and norms, sense of self and space, relationship vs. obligations, mental processes and rewards and recognition, dress and appearance, food and eating habits. |
| 18 | Value structure: goals are the same to ensure that the means of production are used appropriately, that the production process is effective and profitable, and that its results are distributed among members of society. | 23 | Difference between Europe/SEA countries perceived in interpreting the buyer's response and in selecting, modifying, applying, interpreting buyer's behaviour and concepts. |
| 19 | The ins and outs of leadership may very well prove to be the same all over the 184 countries of the world. This is another element adding to the formation of the transcultural world. | | |
| 20 | Daily practice. Some elements, such as the emphasis on product quality and the elimination of status barriers in places like Antines are often similar in Europe | | |

and SEA. However, individual perceptions may still differ.

21 European and Asian markets, like all markets, possess characteristics in common.

22 Natural tendency to misinterpret situations, events, people, and behaviour in other cultures are very similar in Europe and SEA because of subconscious cultural blinkers, lack of cultural awareness and projected similarities coupled with a common tendency to use the Self-Reference Criterion (SRC) when faced with new situations.

23 E/SEA buyers' behaviours are similar in the sense that both are influenced by: product diffusion and adoption characteristics, the market's propensity to change, market standards and the buyer's personal lifestyle.

24 Spoken languages: both Europe and SEA have more than one language and more than one culture plus dialects, accents, slang and jargon.

25 Religion provides meaning and motivation beyond the material aspects of life. It gives meaning to such things as life, what is right and wrong, good and bad. It forms values and attitudes that in turn shape the practices or behaviour of the culture's members. It affects the structure of the educational and economic systems, political organizations and social relations.

26 The lifestyle of both European and SEA societies, cultures/subcultures is the sum of five behavioural aspects:
- the physical development of individuals (nimbleness, dexterity)

24 Communication tools:
- silent language, i.e. gestures, grimaces, posture, colour and distance. Example: European approval is expressed by nodding the head up and down. In the Philippines a jerk of the head downwards means no while a perk upward means yes. A raised thumb is a symbol of approval in Europe. But it is considered very rude in SEA countries.
- spoken language: both groups of languages are generally unknown to the other. Even when a European knows e.g. Malay or Bahasa Indonesian the possibility of misinterpreting a grunt, a hiss or a sigh is high. Nuances associated with choice of words, accent, pattern of speech vary from language to language and within languages; therefore a literal translation is never as good as a rough translation.

25 Beliefs and attitudes in SEA: the major religions are Islam and Buddhism. In Europe, Christianity prevails.

26 Values and norms. From its value system a culture sets norms of behaviour for society, ranging for example, from work ethic to the position of women in society. Therefore, people in Europe and SEA are pleased, concerned, annoyed or embarrassed about different things because they perceive situations differently, e.g. in Europe there is a youth culture; in SEA people venerate old age.

27 Sense of self and space. Feeling comfortable with oneself is influenced by culture. Self-identity, self-worth and self-appreciation can be manifested by a humble or modest bearing in SEA. Europe calls for a sense of independence, assertiveness and creativity compared with group co-operation, harmony and conformity in SEA.

(*Continued*)

| No | Similarities | No | Differences |
|---|---|---|---|
| | – information processing (cognition, perception and logical thought)<br>– the nature of symbolic thought (myths, beliefs, and ritual practices)<br>– social change and innovation, as related to personality (social risk attached to adopting an innovative approach)<br>– role expectations and the socialization of the individual (husband, parent, worker). | 28 | Relationships. Culture establishes relationships on the basis of key factors such as age, sex, power and wisdom as expressed in the family unity. In Europe it is heterogeneous; in SEA, homogeneous. |
| 27 | Tradition and sense of history play a significant role in people's behaviour everywhere. | 29 | Time. Europe: time is an important and valuable commodity (perishable) and there is a need to be precise in many countries. It affects business because "time is money", therefore JV negotiations have to be done within the scheduled time. Time in the year is seen as the four seasons. SEA: time is viewed as circular thus events and opportunities will be repeated just as the monsoon season repeats itself. Time is eternal for them. |
| | | 30 | Mental processes and learning. They are several systems in Europe; they vary from the British (where data, material, objects and other individuals are viewed in terms of a particular goal or result— therefore attention is paid to detail and circumstantial factors) to the French who place general principles ahead of practical considerations. In SEA everything seems to boil down, sooner or later, to social obligations towards the extended family. |
| | | 31 | Rewards and recognition. Manner and methods of offering praise for superior performance and accomplishments vary from testimonial dinners to expense accounts, title and monetary rewards, and they are used differently throughout Europe. The same degree of variance exists in SEA where people are recognized by different rewards. Hence, in cultures such the Javanese in Indonesia, for example, submission is rewarded and valued, which is exactly the opposite of European assertiveness. |
| | | 32 | Dress and appearance and colour. The white of SEA is in glaring contrast to the European black for funeral rites. |

# Appendix No. 6 Trends in Transnational Corporations–Developing Countries Relations: the Confrontation Decades (1950–73)

| No. | Perceived disapproval by | Perceived area of conflict | Policy responses by National Government (NG) or International Bodies (IB) |
|---|---|---|---|
| 1 | Leaders of organized labour | Expansion to foreign markets is a deliberate scheme to subvert wage and employment standards unions have won in the transnational corporations' (TCs) home countries. | Although TCs have great economic power NGs have political and legal powers to ease or to create difficulties to TCs' operations. |
| 2 | Bankers and international monetary authorities | TCs' foreign currency dealings and fund transfers are serious threats to world financial stability. | If and when they have been used instituting new policies or amending existing ones in response to TCs' actions/activities NGs have actually undermined the practicability and profitability of their operations. |
| 3 | Government officials | TCs' transfer of resources and money from country to country is a device to avoid taxes and legal constraints. | |
| 4 | Nationalistic leaders | The spread of TCs is a threat to the economic and political sovereignty of individual nations. | NGs' policies vary from nation to nation and can only be broadly outlined in the following areas:<br>– investment incentives<br>– protection from competition<br>– foreign exchange guarantees<br>– financial assistance<br>– local performance content requirements |
| 5 | General public | TCs' global goals vs. individual host countries' national objectives. To maximize global profitability, TCs disregard individual countries' needs/aspirations or play one against the other. | |

(*Continued*)

| No. | Perceived disapproval by | Perceived area of conflict | Policy responses by National Government (NG) or International Bodies (IB) |
|---|---|---|---|
| 6 | The TCs themselves | Operating at any one time in more than one country reconciling their actions with different and contrasting needs becomes at times an impossible task. | – exporting obligations<br>– limits on foreign payments<br>– technology transfer rules. |
| 7 | International level | Multiplicity of effects any TC's actions has on its home and/or host country(ies) | The first collective policy-response to TCs was made in 1970. It formulated and enacted a far-reaching set of rules governing FDI. |
| 8 | International level | TC's action to achieve a specific goal may thwart achievement of another objective important to its home/host country(ies). | |
| 9 | Balance of payments | TCs aggravate payment deficits. | The 1976 OECD declaration on International Investment and Multinational Enterprises covers virtually all facets of TCs' operations and relationships with home and host countries. |
| 10 | Employment | TCs have been charged with "exporting jobs" from their home countries by transferring resources and operations abroad. | |
| 11 | Economic development | In the post second World War era up to the end of the 1960s TCs contributed to the development of the "third world". Towards the end of the 1960s the rising spirit of nationalism in developing countries changed that perception. Hence the accusations tend to (1) deter the establishment of new enterprises by local investors and entrepreneurs, (2) bring to the developing countries technology too sophisticated (and too capital intensive for local low-skilled, under-employed | The UN Code of Conduct relating to TCs has comprehensive coverage in a serious attempt to construct a solid international legal framework to govern TCs' actions.<br>It aims at fulfilling the need to close the gap between TCs' global reaction and NGs' powers limited to their borders.<br>It has been in the making for over ten years. It has not yet been finalised and/or adopted. |

| No. | Perceived disapproval by | Perceived area of conflict | Policy responses by National Government (NG) or International Bodies (IB) |
|---|---|---|---|
| | | labour force) or obsolete and therefore does not help preparing developing countries to compete effectively in the international market, (3) introduce expensive consumer goods to developing countries, engendering a consumption-oriented value system among the local masses leading to unrest by creating demands that can't be fulfilled, (4) retard economic development because to import consumer products interferes with investments deemed vital to national development. | |

# Appendix No. 7
# Trends in Transnational Corporations–Developing Countries' Relations: the Co-operative Decades (from mid 1970s to beginning of the 1990s)

| FDI/SWINGS implications | Developing countries | Transnational corporations |
|---|---|---|
| – in volume<br>– source from which it flowed<br>– in the host country(ies) in which it flowed<br>– size<br>– structure<br>– increase in the number of industries in which TCs operate | – because more open and less restrictive towards transnational corporations (TCs)<br>– their policies shifted from protection and strict regulation to openness and promotion, deregulation and privatization<br>– their perception of TCs changed from creatures of capitalism to organizations possessing a package of appealing economic attributes<br>– adoption of growth strategy — via export promotion — creating increased linkages to the global economy<br>– TCs were the vehicle to start forging this bond<br>– growing realization that international debt/equity ratios of many developing countries were out of balance<br>– the fixed cost and repayment terms of debts needed to be complemented by more flexible and responsive capital flow requirements | – they include developing countries more often in their global strategies<br>– they welcome this shift in policy — leading from international debts to international equity — partly made also because there was no other choice, additional debt capital was not available<br>– their perception of developing countries has changed from bureaucratic and not business-minded to a potential partner in dialogue and even in business<br>– seeing and witnessing this shift in the business climate, they have become |

| | | |
|---|---|---|
| – increase in the complexity of negotiations between TCs and developing countries creating an<br>– asymmetric and unequal situation in their abilities to evaluate the impact of projects<br>• on achieving their goals<br>• on their ability to organize administratively to undertake most effective negotiations<br>– factors influencing flows:<br>• current account imbalances, debt and capital reserves<br>• changing relations<br>• cost structures | – World Bank's imposition of conditionality clause<br>– effects of TCs' activities in developing countries on:<br>• general • labour • investment<br>• trade • technical efficiency • socio-political aspects<br>• economic structure<br>– change in the external environment of developing countries<br>• trade<br>• technology<br>• cascade effects from initial successful policy shift to TCs by some developing countries<br>• lessons from West and East alliance/competitiveness<br>• learning to live with TCs<br>– change in the internal environment<br>• deregulation/privatization policy designed, and adopted and implemented creating<br>• an increasing number of industries opened to TCs<br>• restrictions on: domestic ownership share/employment of expatriate technicians and managers were abolished<br>– incentives to TCs included<br>• tax relief • tariff protection<br>• accelerated depreciation • overt/disguised export subsidies<br>• loss carry-forward • subsidised infrastructure<br>• manpower training grants<br>– Developing countries began to forcefully promote themselves on the world business scene through:<br>• missions • participating in investment and trade fairs | more willing to accept a certain degree of regulations and laws affecting new operations in any developing country<br>– they are agents of change in developing countries:<br>• economic • political<br>• social • cultural<br>– they push these changes in a definite direction, towards:<br>• openness in the economy<br>• increased link to the internal economic, technical, political environment<br>• a capitalist, consumer-oriented model of development<br>• a more valued-based and less relationship-based way of doing business<br>• a general scientific outlook to life<br>• a shift away from acceptance of authority or divine revelation (beyond individual questioning) towards the individual<br>• an entrepreneurial materialistic culture away from the general static, less materialistic environment of highly traditional developing countries |

(*Continued*)

| FDI/SWINGS Implications | Developing countries | Transnational corporations |
|---|---|---|
| • industrial organization and firm's specific advantage | • opening investment promotion centres<br>• participating/organizing seminars, lectures, etc.<br>– Negotiations with TCs<br>• symmetric for goals, strategies, ownership, local advantages<br>• asymmetric when<br>• its goals are loosely defined and multi-dimensional<br>• its organization structure cannot be easily focused and co-ordinated during negotiations with TCs | • influencing the developing countries societies they operate in via:<br>• the ability to deliver material goods<br>• more willingness to pay for these goods and promoting the advantages of purchasing these goods<br>• they increased their total numbers — coming from more countries and wanted to diversify their portfolio on the world business scene. Thus<br>• their competition sharpened and<br>• their willingness to co-operate increased markedly<br>– Negotiations with developing countries<br>• symmetric for<br>• goals • ownership<br>• strategies • local advantages<br>• asymmetric when<br>• its goals are narrowly defined and one-dimensional<br>• its organizational structure to carry on negotiations with developing countries is sharply focused and co-ordinated. |

# Appendix No. 8
## Sketch of the Seven Historical Stages of the Adaptability Process. Developing Country (Government + Firm) vs. Transnational Corporations (TCs)

| No. | Phases | Host Country Government | Host Country Firm | Foreign TCs |
|---|---|---|---|---|
| 1 | Colonial era | Total dependence on foreign government | Insufficient autonomy to play a critical role in the development | Play a critical role in the use of host country natural resources |
| 2 | Until end of Second World War | Passive acceptance label "underdeveloped" indiscriminately applied to all developing countries and therefore also to Southeast Asian (SEA) countries | Local firms still dominated by foreign firms (TCs) | Continue to play a ruling role in host country |
| 3 | Post Second World War | Labels still apply. Overseas sources of supply begin to be implemented | Local firms have to learn to become self-reliant (awareness process begins) | Their influence begins to show cracks |
| 4 | 1950–60s era | Policies are designed and developed for economic growth. But their labels hardly help them to improve self-image | Local firms begin to assert their independence | TCs continue to nourish feelings of inferiority and inadequacy among local firms instead of eradicating them |

(*Continued*)

| No. | Phases | Host Country Government | Host Country Firm | Foreign TCs |
|---|---|---|---|---|
| 5 | 1960–70s era | Developing countries begin to realize that: (1) undue emphasis on economic growth might lead to lop-sided development; (2) it could stand in the way of the desired social and cultural goals; (3) analysis of socio-cultural impact of economic policies becomes necessary to a comprehensive national policy making | Local firms try to assert their independence but they tend to assume that they cannot be as "efficient", "innovative", or "successful" as the foreign TCs | The influx of FDI led to creation of local entrepreneurs. But TCs still maintain dominant role. The cases of successful economic growth of countries such as Singapore and Malaysia are a case in point |
| 6 | 1970–80s era | Full awareness of 5 above + becoming concerned with international financial situation | Entrepreneurial class undergoes a process of differentiation. New conflicts arise. Some assert their independence, others are still subject to TCs' dominance | They begin to realize old "rules of the game" are changing and with them the investment climate. They try, at different levels, to consider how to adapt. Growth of local entrepreneurial class. They begin to question whether they are able to transform their relationship with host country to their favour |

| | | | | |
|---|---|---|---|---|
| 7 | 1980–90s | Countries in SEA are well set on their path to industrialization and to successful competition with Western/European TCs/industries. Understanding their requirement for continuous sophisticated technology, huge capital investments and access to foreign markets, they redesigned old policies or shaped new policies which on the one hand widely opened doors to TCs, on the other hand regulated their operations to assure a cascade of benefits for their nation. Thus they are able to make their voices heard in world business. | Local TCs begin not only to develop but also to invest in other Southeast Asian countries. Some seek to challenge foreign domination in sectors in which technology has already been standardized, i.e. banking, mining, petroleum, or high-tech, such as microelectronics, and succeed. For them and others of paramount importance is the pace of industrialization and development of national human resources | They try to comply with the newly designed policies and to adapt to the new rules and regulations. In the process different degrees of adaptability emerge because of their attitude and that of their expatriate personnel negotiating in host country |

# Appendix No. 9
# Extending the Globalization Process to Developing Countries via the European Industry. (The 5Ws of the problem + How to solve it) by the European Round Table (ERT)

| No. | Ws | Findings |
|---|---|---|
| 1 | What is the problem? | The problem is:<br>Foreign Direct Investment (FDI) will never be sustainable if it is isolated from, or in confrontation with, the local private sector. Partnership is necessary, and this partnership can occur in two forms: competition according to market rules, or co-operation. For a nation's industry to be internationally competitive, the local enterprises must be exposed to an international level of competition. Moreover, the local economy must be linked to international networks of sourcing and finance, technical intelligence and marketing know-how for local markets and exports. FDI is one way to bring in international competitive pressure, and a way of becoming "plugged into" the global market-place is to become a site for subsidiaries of foreign enterprises. Co-operation becomes an issue between companies when they engage in common enterprises; improvements in conditions for local and foreign private investments should also become something to discuss jointly. |
| 2 | Where is the problem? | The problems as perceived by host countries are:<br>– investors still seem to be *ignorant of the host country's main policies* (imports, taxes, etc.) or to act without adequate information on economic and social factors. Sometimes, the authorities of host countries were surprised to see the slow reaction of foreign businesses to improvements in policies;<br>– some investors were *not always open with the authorities* about their plans, which caused confusion and/or suspicion. Sometimes, the authorities found that the foreigners had no serious intention to invest, or that a longer-term perspective was lacking; |

| No. | Ws | Findings |
|---|---|---|
| | | – authorities in host countries expect foreign investors to *understand the needs of the host country*, to show sufficient interest in areas of priority of the national economy, to be committed to the development of the country, to behave like good corporate citizens and to contribute to improving the localities in which they operate;<br>– *there are still some foreign investors who want to keep local subsidiaries artificially dependent* on their know-how rather than seeing them become self-sufficient; these investors are unwilling to transfer know-how and technology effectively to their local employees;<br>– some investors are suspected of *dumping obsolete equipment* in host countries;<br>– some foreign investors still give too much preference to importing components instead of creating demand upstream;<br>– the gradual *development of linkages* with the host economy is not always a priority with investors. Some local businessmen regard foreign investors as unbeatable competitors, with more advanced technologies and financial resources that risk forcing the local industry out of business;<br>– the authorities know that the problems related to such fears are aggravated when foreign investors are not willing to put *more effort into co-operating* with local businessmen when pursuing their projects;<br>– local business people also complain that multinational companies and their local managers often have better access to host country governments than the local industrialists: ministers listen to foreign discussion partners, but may not take the need of local businesses into account. These local businessmen fear that the changes proposed, or already implemented, in conditions for investment may put local entrepreneurs at a disadvantage;<br>– foreign companies look upon some of the host countries as nothing more than *bags of money to be squeezed*; their priority is on repatriating rather than on reinvesting profits in the country;<br>– some host countries fear that foreign investors will follow preferences for sectors where a monopolistic or oligopolistic situation can be established;<br>– arrogance is a major risk: the fact that some investors tend to look down on their *local labour force* was remarked upon; nor, it was said, do they treat them the way they treat employees in their home country;<br>– foreign investors increase unbalanced urbanization; |

(*Continued*)

| No. | Ws | Findings |
|---|---|---|
| | | – foreign investors are not truly interested in solving *environmental problems* and avoiding waste and pollution. Developing countries are said to be the preferred locations for building dangerous factories (toxic waste, health hazards to the labour force and the surrounding population). |
| 3 | When will the remaining impediments to investors be solved? | The remaining impediments to FDI will be solved when:<br>– bureaucracy and ad hoc state interference are replaced by legislation and a more liberal attitude. There is some resistance to change among bureaucrats the world over, even if their governments want to change. There is still a tendency to work and decide case by case (e.g. on permits for investment), which gives more power to the bureaucracy and—let's be honest—opens the door to corruption;<br>– conditions under which a country's exports can compete in the world's markets will be created; otherwise the result will inevitably be more bureaucracy and more regulations;<br>– some governments will be confident enough to embrace the market economy fully, to give full recognition to the positive role that the private sector in general, and FDI in particular, could play in their development process;<br>– some *restrictions on sectorial access* will be lifted. In an increasing number of countries, this concerns only basic public services, while in other countries, foreign investors are banned from producing strategic raw materials or selected manufactured goods;<br>– cultural and mental particularities, habits and traditions of a country will not be forgotten by foreign investors. As industrialists we should try to be more sensitive to such issues so as to understand these countries better. The world cannot be defined by financial ratios and figures alone. The cultural and social background plays a more important role as part of the individual life, part of politics, part of business and the economy;<br>– the risk of re-regulation through the back door will no longer be a risk. Uncompetitive local industrialists may press for the reintroduction of sectorial licensing in order to keep more dynamic competitiors at bay;<br>– some *restrictions on foreign ownership* will no longer persist;<br>– enforcement of intellectual property rights will no longer be relatively weak and obtaining a patent—when transferring foreign technology—will no longer involve a long, complicated procedure;<br>– other difficulties (isolated leftovers of old and inefficient institutional structures—some in the capital cities, and, to a very large extent, in rural areas) will be solved. |

| No. | Ws | Findings |
|---|---|---|
| 4 | Why do these impediments persist? | Reasons why these impediments to FDI persist:<br>– *the historical background and the economic situation of host countries*: several host countries mentioned that investors and those asking for liberalization did not know enough about the historical background to the economic conditions and attitudes they might encounter. Cultural differences (sometimes differences in language, even among English-speaking countries) are often underestimated. Some of the least-developed countries in our sample emphasize that the limited resources of host countries should not put a stop to further negotiations at mid-point, but rather lead to smaller-scale partnerships that encourage their local private sectors;<br>– *undone homework on the part of European authorities*:<br>• the impact of EU protectionism directed against the free inflow of goods, services and capital is of interest to European industrialists investing abroad;<br>• there are EU-wide impediments as well and one should be aware of the risks related to the new, relatively far-reaching and interventionist competences of the EU in the Maastricht Treaty, which cover areas such as social policy, industrial policy, technology policy, health, environment and consumer protection. |
| 5 | Who has to deal with these problems? | These problems have to be faced by:<br>– European governments and the European Commission who are not yet paying enough attention to the need to change internal and international economic policies arising from increased globalization and the opening of markets in the developing work. The regional focus of EU external economic policies needs to be adjusted. Measures need to be taken to open the EU markets further, to take the global impact of EU policies more into account, and to support the development and implementation of global rules;<br>– Europeans who have to do their own homework on liberalization better; they need to support opening markets abroad and to remain competitive and credible;<br>– all those who are demanding/suggesting a lot of things to developing countries and are not actually putting them into practice in Europe;<br>– all those who benefit from the quality and the momentum of liberalization. They are:<br>• international investors (among them the companies of the ERT), as new opportunities and the need for rapid reaction come to light;<br>• European industry as a whole, since greater efficiency in the developing world also means intensified competition; |

(*Continued*)

| No. | Ws | Findings |
|---|---|---|
| | | • European authorities, for globalization and liberalization should force them to look beyond Europe's domestic economic scene even more than before; and<br>• host countries in the developing world (and possibly also in Eastern Europe) to help them shape their future policies. |
| 6 | How will these problems be resolved? | These problems will be faced and resolved by:<br>– adopting an overall positive attitude towards liberalization of international trade which means implementing the GATT, finalizing the Uruguay Round and then building momentum to continue negotiations for liberalizing the world economy further;<br>– the primary requisites for increasing FDI-*domestic confidence* and *authentic competitiveness*;<br>– instead of a proliferation of regulations that cause progressive strangulation, liberalization and *gains in efficiency* continue under their own momentum. Not only does this result in increased demand, but *new competitors* are also emerging. Companies will have to take these factors into account;<br>– *pragmatism and relevance* which are more important to an efficient policy than theoretical purity. Transforming the economy must be an internal process, responsive to national aspirations, carried out under national leadership, following the priorities defined in a national long-term strategy. International competition on rules is, in our opinion, the most efficient way of improving the general economic setting of a country and of refocusing public policy. Completing this internal process of transformation successfully also requires *commitment* from decision-makers and the major social groups in the country concerned and a will to change. Competition on rules will rapidly unmask mere window-dressing;<br>– companies have to develop *practical solutions to alleviate local anxieties*; and they have to find ways to overcome the imperfections of local markets and to alleviate risks. The necessary adaptations have to be developed on a case-by-case basis but should include two generally applicable principles: partnership and long-term thinking. Specific agreements negotiated with the authorities of host countries are one of several solutions that take local particularities and fears into account;<br>– host countries have the right to expect *good citizenship* from investors and honest co-operation with the government. Each company has to integrate itself completely. In addition, active efforts at co-operation may also be undertaken by groups of industries. |

# Appendix No. 10
# Not Just Cultural Tips for European Businessmen Looking to Southeast Asia

| General | Indonesia | Thailand | Vietnam |
|---|---|---|---|
| 1. Friendship first, business second. Avoid overfamiliarity. Be polite formally. Emotional restraint is imperative. | 1. The assumption in Europe is that Indonesian companies, especially the large conglomerates with strong government ties, are often thought to operate in a culture of corruption. Be open minded. | 1. Western education is popular among Thais and can help reduce language and cultural barriers. | 1. Vietnam, even by Asian standards, is a country of rules and no rules, passion and a lot of improvisation. |
| 2. Make it a long-term commitment. | 2. Meetings are seen as forums for airing problems, not necessarily solving them and one-to-one meetings are unusual, initiating the process and camaraderie are essential. | 2. The majority of Thais are Buddhist. They avoid aggression, respect status and seniority, are tolerant and revere relationships. | 2. Vietnam corporate decision making is very hierarchical, authoritarian and can be lengthy. But if European companies comply with instructions, action is swift. |
| 3. Be aware of dignity and avoid confrontation. | 3. Consensus is vital. | 3. Westerners who only look as far as the next deal and avoid becoming part of the family will miss out. | 3. Business cards are popular and should be offered with the right hand; business meetings should only be arranged two to three weeks in advance and small gifts are usual for the principal hosts. |
| 4. Be patient. | 4. Agreement is necessary from boards of commissioners, | 4. Smiles and "small talk" are common and important. | |
| 5. Be informed. | | 5. Just because no one is disputing what you say, does not mean they agree with you. | |
| 6. Respect age and seniority. | | | |
| 7. Temper the use of Western logic. | | | |
| 8. Cultivate contacts—family, friends and business. | | | |
| 9. Seek formal introductions. | | | |
| 10. Assume English is not properly understood. | | | |

*(Continued)*

| General | Indonesia | Thailand | Vietnam |
|---|---|---|---|
| 11. Learn a local language.<br>12. Appoint a distributor with a recognized status and influence.<br>13. Persevere in knocking at the same right doors.<br>14. Be persistent.<br>15. Have a visible presence in the chosen Southeast Asian market keeping in personal contact with potential customers. | usually consisting of community members and maybe government members.<br>5. Those of you who seek to influence the executive management of the company, the public owners of the company and the beneficiaries of the company (who may or may not own any share of the company), are likely to be considered astute and worth doing business with.<br>6. Perseverance, never lose your serene enthusiasm.<br>7. Never lose your temper.<br>8. Develop an Indonesian way to get feedback from your staff who might at the beginning be unwilling to ask questions. | 6. Sino-Thais dominate in business, but they are less likely to rely on the Chinese family-style management. However, decisions are still rarely made in a systematic Western fashion.<br>7. Companies should not judge situations on strictly Western criteria. It is not by accident that the most successful foreign companies in Thailand usually have Thai general managers. | 4. There is almost no distinction between business and personal life in Vietnam, so be prepared for almost continual contact with customers and partners, even outside the office. |

# Appendix No. 11
# Tips for Planning Markets Penetration Strategies

| No. | Planning tips | No. | Planning tips |
|---|---|---|---|
| 1 | Have specific proposals and contingency plans—and then plan, plan and plan. | 17 | You need to be strong financially. The bond requirements and penalty clauses are extremely onerous. |
| 2 | Get to know your potential partner and take account of his long-term objectives. Establish clear strategic leadership but learn flexible management. | 18 | If you don't have contacts in the area, then make use of the EU services on offer. |
| 3 | Accommodate cultural differences—but not at the cost of the financial bottom line. | 19 | Can you produce a competitive bid? Pre-tender research is essential. |
| 4 | Orchestrate technology transfer—to your own agenda and pace and learn from a local partner's strengths. | 20 | Have a tender strategy. Some decide to provide a competitive price and to consider the politics. Others include local companies in the package. |
| 5 | Recognize that there are short- and long-term time horizons, that both result in different ground rules and values when compared with the West, but that profit is universal. | 21 | Remember that Conditions of Contract are very onerous and not subject to negotiation. (For example, contracts are fixed price and lump sum only.) |
| 6 | View the region as a programme, not on a one-off basis. | 22 | Post-tender negotiations can be expensive. Some take months. |
| 7 | Use Asian advisors. | 23 | Learn quickly when and how to wait without despairing. |
| 8 | Find local partners, but on an equal basis. Localize prudently. | 24 | Don't leap in the dark. The more you plan the more successful your action will be. |
| 9 | Recognize cultural differences. | 25 | The more your actual/potential partner sees your know-how to balance, respect, trust and self-interest the more you will be appreciated. |
| 10 | Respect dignity and age. | 26 | Learn how to listen, when to speak and how. |
| 11 | Forget whose backyard you are in. | | |
| 12 | Take credit ratings or stock market valuations at face value. | | |
| 13 | Forget that yesterday's leaders lead to losses. | | |
| 14 | Are you fully prepared to tender for a major contract? | | |
| 15 | Is the project suitable for your firm? | | |
| 16 | Can you afford the tender costs? Some tenders take one year to prepare. It can be a drain on senior management, and failure can have a traumatic effect. | | |

# Appendix No. 12
# The Structure of the European Construction Industry (A Bird's-eye View)

| No. | Areas |
|---|---|
| 1 | CONSTRUCTION OUTPUT as percentage of GDP is 7–8 per cent of EU countries |
| 2 | THE SECTOR IS CHARACTERIZED BY:<br>— A highly volatile demand for its products. Changes to take place suddenly and with little warning.<br>— Professionals in the sector expect that as the single market becomes more of a practical reality, EU funds will be used to create trans-European networks of transport, telecommunications and energy infrastructures mainly intended for Spain, Portugal, Ireland and Greece.<br>— There is a steady, long-term decline in the demand for direct, site-based construction work—traditionally the work base for contractors.<br>— There are 1.5 m contractors employing 2.6 m people. Very often they have informal close links with one or two contractors for whom they do most of their work. They are very small, i.e. about four people.<br>— The top 20 firms have a turnover of a minimum of 2039 million ECU in Spain to a maximum of 9228 million ECU (Bouygues in France). The top 35 contractors have an average turnover of 1250 million ECU at 1991 prices.<br>— Big contractors consist of separate divisions each organized like a medium-sized contractor.<br>— The majority of them operate in only one local market.<br>— To survive most of them must remain flexible so as to be able to respond to the level and pattern of demand. Thus they (1) try to avoid becoming capital intensive (2) tend to subcontract work and ownership of plant and equipment (3) invest as little as possible in training, feedback systems and R&D.<br>— The career firms are mainly based in larger EU countries (UK 8, France 7 and Germany 3).<br>— The biggest contractors are part of a group of companies working in several industries of which construction is just one. |
| 3 | JOINT VENTURES<br>— They are increasingly common in bids for major projects (Channel Tunnel, Jubilee Line in London, etc.) within Europe but not to the same extent overseas and not in SEA in particular. |

| No. | Areas |
|---|---|
| | — Many believe that new opportunities are to be found through JVs, strategic alliances, mergers, acquisitions and general co-operation. However, there were 198 intra-European mergers and acquisitions amongst contractors in 1991. The number fell to 86 in 1992.<br>— A preview of things to come has been the formation of the Société Européenne de Construction (SEC), a joint company set up in Brussels by Laing (UK), Dumer (France), MCC (Sweden) and Strabag (Germany), with an annual turnover of ECU 11 billion and 94 000 employees. |
| 4 | FINANCIAL<br>— In some EC countries (Germany, Spain and France), contractors have institutionalized links with industrial banks.<br>— Medium-size contractors (i.e. 250 to 1250 million ECU turnover) are—by and large—financially weak.<br>— The financing of infrastructure projects is more complex than in earlier times and contractors are increasingly expected to help find finance for new constructions, which increases the risks they face not having European-wide facilities to boost their competitiveness in the international market-place.<br>— Weaknesses: the volatility of demand makes it difficult for contractors to plan ahead and so restrict the amount they can afford to invest in developing their own efficiency and competence especially in training and R&D. Thus they adopt a very short-term view to cope with fluctuating load and the demands of shareholders for regular and consistent dividends. These weaknesses mean contractors consider financing a major problem, banks discriminate against them charging very high interest rates because they are contractors and also small (with profits rarely exceeding 2–3 years of turnover). |
| 5 | IMAGE<br>— Contractors suffer—by and large—from a poor image and a poor reputation both with customers and with society at large because of past failures in technology, delivery performance, poor quality and claims for more money. Contractors tend not to see issues from customers' point of view. |
| 6 | COMPETITION<br>— The fragmented approach of the industry makes it difficult for contractors to ensure they are paid for their work on time. This is the ultimate result of cut-throat competition which makes their attitudes towards customers aggressive rather than conciliatory.<br>— The sector is characterized by ineffective marketing. This limits demand for construction and exasperates competiton.<br>— Architectural and engineering consultants do not collaborate with contractors. As a result, they accuse contractors of caring only about maximising profits and not about quality. |
| 7 | MANAGEMENT<br>— Lack of competent management in many sectors of the industry. Thus:<br>— Contractors are not involved in ensuring that their needs are reflected in basic professional education.<br>— The education and training of contractors has to be reviewed using the standards achieved by Germany. |

(*Continued*)

| No. | Areas |
|---|---|
| 8 | CONSULTANTS<br>— Architects and design engineers represent a strategic advantage of the EU construction industry in the international market-place.<br>— However, this strategic advantage remains an almost untapped potential.<br>— Within the EU contractors and designers have often devoted their energies to confrontation and not finding ways and means for a sound long-term harmonious relationship.<br>— Outside the EU European designers/consultants are in demand but only a regrettably negligible number of EU-based contractors exploit this competitive advantage to the full.<br>— A number of contractors aiming at controlling the total construction process have started buying design consultancy firms and have also improved efficiency as a spin-off.<br>— Information flow about the performance of construction facilities in use is still a problem in the contractors' approach to design.<br>— Contractors needing to take responsibility for improving construction work do not produce newsworthy ideas for improving both their structure and their image. |

*Source*: Basic information from EU Commission DG III—Industry.

# Appendix No. 13
# Similarities and Differences in the EU Construction Industries

| No. | Similarities | No. | Differences |
|---|---|---|---|
| 1 | There are relatively few issues which are common problems to all EU Member States | 1 | Between each Member State in legal systems, context construction processes |
| 2 | There are few European solutions | 2 | Differences in the present market situation of Member States |
| 3 | The most important aspect is not to eliminate difference but harmonization | 3 | The EU legal system in Member States is divided into two camps:<br>(a) Anglo-Saxon common law (UK and Ireland) with no underlying civil code relies little on regulations and heavily on interventionist and market approaches<br>(b) Roman Law relies heavily on regulations and little on market approaches but — it is alleged — encourages evasion of overcomplex regulations |
| 4 | There are regional similarities in climate, culture, tradition, family structure, labour market and similar forces | 4 | Firms in Anglo-Saxon countries of the EU want to see a clearer institutional framework with registration of firms, more qualifications, a simpler set of contract forms etc. to be recognized in the rest of the EU |
| 5 | EU professionals in the industry are afraid of solutions imposed by EU directives which may be in their view:<br>– unnecessary<br>– inappropriate<br>– the cause of unequal burdens of implementation | 5 | Firms in the Roman-law countries of the EU want to see more flexible approaches spread throughout the EU |
| 6 | *Competition between countries* within the EU is forcing a streamlining of attitudes | 6 | *Market differences* exist between the different markets within the EU. Some of them are:<br>(1) in the Southern States (i.e. Portugal, Greece, Ireland, Southern Italy) where infrastructure needs are greatest and are: (a) met by dependency on the EU structural funds; |
| 7 | *Image of the whole industry*: bad. This creates problems throughout the EU in:<br>(a) attracting potential customers and new recruits;<br>(b) promoting the role the sector has to play in building Europe;<br>(c) selling the benefits of new construction to improve productivity, health and lifestyle;<br>(d) promoting the advantages of new technologies;<br>(e) taking an aggressive lead in offering excellent guarantees of its work and products;<br>(f) avoiding defensive fights for protection from liability claims | | |

(*Continued*)

| No. | Similarities | No. | Differences |
|---|---|---|---|
| 8 | Fragmentation: the 1.5m firms in the sector contribute to:<br>(a) volatility of output which causes short-term attitudes, problems of planning, recruitment, training, investment and research<br>(b) information deficiencies in the market for contracting and designing—territorial battles<br>(c) (a) and (b) above lead to cut-throat competition, which breeds short-term attitudes and lack of investment<br>(d) tendering procedures in which technical merit is still judged after price | | (b) attracting interest from contractors from the rest of the EU and beyond; (c) stimulating the competitiveness of their own contractors who have considerable export know-how gained in North Africa, Middle East and former colonies<br>(2) in Germany there is the special problem of rebuilding former East Germany and its financial difficulties. The construction standards, performance, quality and reliability of contractors' work enjoy outstanding international reputations |
| 9 | Lack of diversification in products find market's increasing dependence on a single geographical market area | | (3) Denmark and Holland have fewer infrastructure needs and look forward to substantially increasing their export capabilities. They have a comparative advantage in high quality, high technology, civil engineering and building |
| 10 | Ways to gain work: contractor bids too low to gain work and then:<br>(a) reduces quality or<br>(b) relies on variations to the contract and claims to increase the price but<br>(c) is caught out by rising input prices and<br>(d) suffers from very low or no profits at all or<br>(e) is unable to complete the work | | (4) UK and Ireland have highly cyclical construction markets<br>(5) of all EU Member States only Germany applies a long-term philosophy to the sector. In UK and Ireland, stock market forces dictate a short-term philosophy. The other EU Member States cannot afford/do not believe in the long-term approach (except Denmark and Holland) |
| 11 | R&D: only a few big firms give appropriate attention to R&D. For many others it is almost negligible. Thus:<br>(a) skill shortages when demand increases<br>(b) poor understanding of the behaviour of complex constructions | 7 | The roles participants/players in the construction sector have to play are the consequence of:<br>(a) historical differences<br>(b) differences in legal systems |
| 12 | Long-term relationships: they seem to be the domain of those contractors who see loyalty and continuity of demands as competitive advantage. But they operate in specific market niches. As a result, they tend to be financially strong, but they are not—on the whole—representative of the 1.5 million EU contractors | 8 | *Climate and topography* dictate:<br>(a) different technical regulations and standards<br>(b) different methods, materials and products |
| | | 9 | The portion of *repair and maintenance* activity |
| | | 10 | Characteristics of the *housing market* |

| No. | Similarities | No. | Differences |
|---|---|---|---|
| 13 | Overcoming discrepancies: throughout the EU construction industry, there is a need to overcome discrepancies between:<br>(a) client and construction team<br>(b) professions<br>(c) trades in which factory manufacturing is inappropriate<br>(d) contractor and sub-contractor<br>There is a need for communication standards and a need for training support and information services for medium–small firms and the lack of it. | 11 | *Specialist technologies*: the major differences are:<br>– France (nuclear power cons.)<br>– Scotland and Norway (offshore construction)<br>– Germany (cladding systems)<br>– The Netherlands (water engineering)<br>– Finland (pre-fabricated concrete structures)<br>– Italy (dams, tunnels, bridges) |
| | | 12 | *Education and training*: the very different EU Member States individual systems create barriers to dissemination of technology. These problems create: |
| | | 13 | *Differences in the adoption of any new innovations.* Thus national traditions in construction change slowly and an EU tradition only emerges with difficulty. |
| | | 14 | *New standards and planning regulations*: point (13) above creates serious differences and difficulties in:<br>(a) the level of co-ordination of research and development<br>(b) the effectiveness of new standards and planning regulations. |

*Source*: Basic information from EU Commission DG III—Industry.

# Appendix No. 14 The International Construction Industry (A Comparative Bird's-eye View)

| FUNCTION | JAPAN | USA | EUROPE |
|---|---|---|---|
| 1. Total number of contractors | 510 000 | 1.9 m | 1.5 m |
| 2. Total number of employees | 5.8 m | 6.7 m | 7.6 m |
| 3. Total number of independent workers | included in employees | 1.5 m | 1.3 m |
| 4. Average size of contractor (people) | 11.5 | 4.9 | 4 |
| 5. Contracts awarded to firms from the international competition (1992) | 17 contracts to US companies totalling 120 m ECU | In 1991 USA firms undertook 11 billion ECU's worth of work in the EU region | The total amount of EU's contractors in Japan and USA is negligible compared with the volume of work they generate inside Europe. Most contractors fear losing EU construction work to them. Example in 1991: the UK attracted 12 per cent of all Japanese foreign investments in Europe. Since Japanese contractors have long relationships with these investors, construction work was given to them. |

| Function | Japan | USA | Europe |
|---|---|---|---|
| 6. Marketing staff of the top 10 firms | More than 7000 full-time professionals (or a maximum of 40 per cent of staff) | About 30 per cent of staff devote their full-time efforts on marketing on a global scale | No significant professional investment in effective marketing in general and in particular not at all comparable to Japan or USA firms' efforts |
| 7. Value of contracts to firms awarded overseas (outside their own country) (1995) | ECU 2 billion or 15 per cent of global market share (GMS) | US$ 75 billion or 39% per cent of global market share | The leading countries for overseas work are: France, 9.2 per cent GMS; Germany, 6.5 per cent GMS; Italy, 6.8 per cent GMS and the UK, 12.4 per cent GMS. Their work overseas amount to 5–10 per cent of their total turnover |
| 8. Most important strategic competitive advantages at home and in overseas markets | (1) Financial engineering in general and for high risk projects in particular<br>(2) To provide technical assistance on complex projects<br>(3) Penetration of a new market is routinely preceded by an in-depth study period by senior executives based in the market to be conquered with the simple objective of | (1) Political clout<br>(2) Financial engineering<br>(3) Reputation for fast track construction<br>(4) Dominance in process plant construction<br>(5) Outstanding international reputation<br>(6) Effective strategic marketing<br>(7) Ability to think and act strategically to achieve critical mass and not just chase jobs around the world | – Europe has a range of strengths across many disciplines.<br>– However, the competitive advantages that exist in the EU today are very arbitrary and diverse<br>– Technologies have developed for various reasons and compete at different levels appropriate to their application<br>– Knowledge and skills needed for advanced construction technologies does not lag behind Japan and USA |

(*Continued*)

| Function | Japan | USA | Europe |
|---|---|---|---|
| | (a) listening;<br>(b) learning<br>(4) Negotiating abilities | | – However, the fragmented markets, the volatility of the demand organizational financial engineering and lower level of commitment than that of USA and Japan allows Europe to give a competitive advantage to its international competitors<br>– EU's contractors are better than US or Japanese contractors at creating and building attractive architectural environments |
| 9. R&D | – Funded by the big six through high profile institutes which carry out research on long-term visionary topics (robotization, space structures, seismic control etc.)<br>– Promoted through Kaizen culture (or small technical improvements) by workers at all levels<br>– Total investment 2.9 per cent of GNP | – Promoted and funded by national institutions, i.e. construction industry institutions, civil engineering, research foundation, etc.<br>– As spin-off in certain technologies from federal defense and energy programmes<br>– Dominance in process plant construction<br>– Financial strength of major firms (F. Daniels, Bechtel, etc.) controlling several EU players<br>– Total investment 2.8 per cent of GNP<br>– Funded by the big contractors | – Germany takes a long-term view on research which allows it to think in terms of management philosophy and networks of values shared by thousands of small and medium-sized firms. At the core of this cluster of values there are two qualities: a passionate desire for independence and fascination with technology. These values have deep cultural roots. Thus the firms in the construction sector are good at focusing and co-ordinating R&D |

| Function | Japan | USA | Europe |
|---|---|---|---|
| | | | – France, the UK, Italy and less wealthy countries are progressively less good at it<br>– EU construction R&D is very fragmented, with little communication between: (a) research bodies in different EU Member States; (b) governments, universities and industry research centres<br>– Total investment varies from 0.5 per cent to 2.9 per cent of EU Member States' GNP<br>– Most of the construction R&D is funded by the materials and building products supply industry. Contractors and consultants give little — in comparison with their share of the activity. |
| 10. Product and material prices (1992) | – Rank below the top 4 EC countries | – Rank above the bottom 3 EU countries | – Not significantly different from Japan and USA |
| 11. Project costs | – No real cost efficiency differences with the EU and USA | – No real cost efficiency differences with the EU and Japan | – On the whole no real cost efficiency differences with Japan and USA. Differences more within different EU regions |
| 12. Major competitive disadvantage | The EU does not have any contractors as big and powerful in financial engineering as the top ten firms in USA and Japan. As civil and heavy engineering construction works are served by large contractors, EU's contractors are at a distinct disadvantage. This competitive disadvantage in competing with the world's best twenty companies can be overcome only by joint ventures and strategic alliances. Yet today there seems to be only one major attempt in Europe to solve this problem: Société Européenne de Construction. | | |

*Source*: Basic data from EU Commission DG III — Industry.

# Appendix No. 15
# Summary of Elements of Strategy by Subsector

**OPTIONS FOR ACTION BY FIRMS:**
- do more and better marketing: understand client needs
- provide financial engineering
- offer a complete product: design, construct, maintain
- integrate design, performance measurement, feedback
- invest in R&D and promote new ideas
- take the initiative in offering good guarantees
- develop technologies needed for the growing environmental market: land reclamation, recycling, decommissioning, transport management
- create mergers and alliances to form a number of world class major construction firms
- develop franchising methods to enable small firms to provide a professional service to customers
- improve health and safety, and implement the requirements of the Construction Sites Directive
- improve training

**ACTION BY INDUSTRY COLLECTIVELY:**
- actively promote EC standards, and argue for high standards
- promote a common EC system of registration and qualification
- take the initiative in promoting a common effective method of dispute resolution
- promote ways to encourage good selection of contractors on the basis of quality, practical design suggestions, life cycle costs, and guarantees
- assist firms to develop and implement health and safety plans as required by the Construction Sites Directive
- promote a positive image for the industry through TV, films, and the press, to improve the volume and standard of recruitment

**ACTION BY GOVERNMENTS EU INSTITUTIONS:**
- introduce mutually recognised registration of contractors
- provide harmonized export credit facilities
- act as model clients to motivate innovation, quality and good procurement practices
- make long-term infrastructure investment plans and stick to them, to stabilize demand and allow the industry to take a long-term view
- set up financial mechanisms to provide seed capital financing for private sector infrastructure projects: create an economic environment in which privately financed infrastructure can grow
- establish widely used and fair forms of contracts
- improve education for construction
- set high levels of European standards and technical regulations
- support R&D

*Source*: EU Commission DG III—Industry

# Appendix No. 16
# Sixteen Priority Steps To Be Taken By A European Construction Firm In Order To Effectively Penetrate The Southeast Asian Market (An Approach for The Future)

| No. | Steps |
|---|---|
| 1 | If the European construction firm does not have the required clout to effectively compete (i.e. size—in terms of turnover and employees—corporate culture and powerful financial muscle), it is better to remain within the EU. |
| 2 | Before effective penetration of new markets in Southeast Asia an in-depth study must ensue in the country whose markets are targeted. (Ambassadors of the European firm—who have to have previous Asia experience—have only one job to do: listen, learn and develop a sound and reliable network of human contacts.) |
| 3 | Translate the business climate and cross-cultural issues/problems encountered into a language easily understandable by the people/decision-makers back home. |
| 4 | Provide technical assistance to key institutions/organizations in the market to be penetrated. |
| 5 | Drawing from the established network of contacts and long-term relationships identify speculative development projects for which finance is needed. |
| 6 | Be prepared to avoid tendering procedures if possible. |
| 7 | Be prepared to experience cut-throat conditions. |
| 8 | Be prepared to compete with the top five USA firms, the big six Japanese, the Koreans and Taiwanese, and their objectives. |
| 9 | Financial engineering. Be prepared to develop a strategy based on reputation and financial strength. This implies organizing a financial package (in Europe) of proposals hard to beat, which means the European construction firm has to act as a guarantor. |
| 10 | This guarantee has to be backed up by a letter of credit provided by a major bank/consortia of banks in Europe willing to lend on favourable terms. |
| 11 | Points 9 and 10 above are sufficient to secure finance from local concerns syndicated to local participants. |
| 12 | Once financing has been arranged secure the contract by knowing how to negotiate: (a) across cultures, (b) on the basis of estimated construction costs. |

*(Continued)*

| No. | Steps |
|---|---|
| 13 | Subcontract to one of the local companies with which you have developed a friendly relationship. |
| 14 | Be sure in planning your activities to including a training component. |
| 15 | Throughout all these steps cultivate effective lobbying to maintain the European export credit advantage. This financial package that Europe makes available to European exporting joint ventures will allow the European enterprises to face minimal risk exposure and financial obstacles as a consequence of exporting. |
| 16 | If all the above steps are carefully and skilfully implemented in the targeted market (in the spirit of daily action) it is possible to gain a competitive advantage on the basis of which effective strategic market penetration can continue. |

# Appendix No. 17
# Joint Ventures in Developing Countries vs. developed Countries An Overview of The 5Ws + Hows (Insights from Joint Venture History)

| Question | Developing countries | Developed countries |
|---|---|---|
| 1. What are joint ventures (JVs)? | The proven mechanism to acquire developed countries, technology | – Transnational corporations' (TCs) dominant form of business in developing countries/host country/ developed countries |
| 2. Why are they important? | Because (a) it is a vehicle to enter the world business stage, (b) to generate cascades of multiple effects on itself, (c) encouragement received by international organizations, i.e. World Bank, UNCTC, OECD, etc. | – development of new industries<br>– revitalization of mature industries<br>– rationalization of a firm's portfolio<br>– the enhancement of a firm's competitive advantage<br>– development of new technologies, i.e. robotics, genetics, engineering, solar energy, fibre optics, etc.<br>– advantage offered in host country |
| 3. How long do they last? | – as long as the partners' commitment lasts | – JVs rarely last long in industries that are subject to volatile competition<br>– firms must devise arrangements to get in and out of ventures before their knowledge becomes obsolete<br>– as long as the partners' commitment lasts |
| 4. What is the danger of a possible JV failure? | – magnify the cost of JV failure because of the declining share of FDI flows from industrialized Western countries to developing countries | – reconfirming the old TCs' assumption of staying away from developing countries<br>– have to face tangible and intangible costs associated with an early dissolution not previously anticipated |

(*Continued*)

| Question | Developing countries | Developed countries |
|---|---|---|
| | – have to face tangible and intangible costs associated with an early dissolution not previously anticipated<br>– face the fact that the JVs' specific long-term needs have not been properly identified and met, by recruiting the foreign partner just on paper | – face the fact that the JVs' specific long-term needs have not been properly identified and met by recruiting the local host country firm, just on paper |
| 5. When to establish a JV? | Whenever the following conditions are met:<br>– a sound need assessed in terms of:<br>• relative importance of each partners' contributions in terms of<br>• capital<br>• knowledge<br>• staff<br>– commitment assessed in terms of:<br>• JV structure<br>• commitment of TC partner to international business<br>• particular venture<br>• particular partner<br>– after a rigorous, systematic partner's search<br>– after expectations are clearly spelled out and clarified<br>– using local managers who have JV equity<br>– shared decision-making (all major issues)<br>– continuous commitment to human investment in maintaining and developing relations with JV partner | Whenever the following conditions are met:<br>– a sound need assessed in terms of:<br>• relative importance of each other partners' contributions in terms of<br>• capital<br>• knowledge<br>• staff<br>– commitment assessed in terms of:<br>• commitment of local partner to international contracts/JV<br>• particular venture<br>• particular partner<br>– after a rigorous, systematic search for a partner<br>– after expectations are voiced and clarified<br>– using local managers who have JV equity<br>– shared decision-making on all major problems<br>– continuous commitment to human investment in maintaining and developing relationship with partner |
| 6. What does it mean to enter a JV agreement? | – to exploit an opportunity for:<br>• acquiring new technology<br>• developing human resources<br>• entering a foreign market<br>• increase national exports | – to expand a network of business units that TCs use to cope with worldwide competition in domestic market |

| Question | Developing countries | Developed countries |
|---|---|---|
| 7. What are the draw-backs of JVs? | – problems created by owner(s)' inability to manage venture by having confidence/trust in local general manager<br>– problems created by foreigner in adapting to host country's culture<br>– conflicts of sovereignty | – antitrust problems<br>– conflicts regarding loss of autonomy and control<br>– loss of competitive advantage through strategic inflexibility<br>– problems created by owners' inability to manage cross-cultural problems and ventures effectively |
| 8. Where is the JV successful? | – at the meeting point—on the performance road—where both partners agree on overall satisfaction<br>– wherever partners' needs and commitment fit well with the JV's performance in<br>• using local managers<br>• using JV structure willingly<br>• TC using local partner for knowledge of the local economy, politics, culture, customs | – achievement of major goals<br>– complementary con-tributions by partners<br>– combining contributions of partners<br>– entry of a smaller and medium-size company<br>– conversion of a licensing agreement and manage-ment contracts as part of a JV agreement |
| 9. When is the JV a failure? | whenever there are:<br>– unresolved performance difficulties which are costly in terms of:<br>• capital<br>• time<br>• social costs to the host country<br>– conflict situations as described in the developed countries column which become unresolved. Yet most of these conflicts are of a cross-cultural nature | – TC global integration, local partner national orientation<br>– perception of unequal benefits and costs<br>– the JV contract does not specify goals of each party, resources to be contributed by the partners, their major responsibilities and obligations, the rights and other key aspects of the JV<br>– TC resources contribution to JV decline<br>– frequent drastic currency fluctuations<br>– conflicts over marketing<br>– transfer pricing conflicts, i.e. purchase of materials, components of the JV from a TC intermediary etc. |

(*Continued*)

| Question | Developing countries | Developed countries |
|---|---|---|
| | | – conflicts over decision-making, managerial processes and style |
| 10. How JVs differ? | – stability<br>– performance<br>– equity<br>– shared decisions<br>– rationale for creating JV<br>– frequency of government partner and autonomy | – stability<br>– performance<br>– ownership<br>– control<br>– rationale for creating JV<br>– frequency of governing partner and autonomy |
| 11. What is the role of the JV general manager? | a key role in determining the success/failure of the JV | a key role in determining the success/failure of the JV |
| 12. What does managing a JV imply? | a balancing act between<br>– parents' priorities<br>– JV's operating priorities<br>– personal objectives, beliefs and values of the expatriate managers representing the JV shareholder | a balancing act between<br>– parents' priorities<br>– JV's strategic priorities on the world business stage<br>– personal objectives, beliefs and values of managers representing the shareholder |
| 13. What is the best attitude of a JV general manager? | one seeks to satisfy: he reaches compromises perceived to be acceptable by the JV partners on:<br>– growth vs. return on investment vs. dividends<br>– long term<br>– gentleness/aggressiveness of the criteria<br>– undefined growth targets vs. growth in sales<br>– the parents' attitude towards the role of the JV general manager on:<br>• source/scope of his authority<br>• status<br>• personality vs. position<br>• responsibility for decision-making<br>• responsibility for future events | one that seeks to satisfy: he reaches compromises perceived to be accepted by the JV partners on:<br>– growth vs. return on investment vs. dividends<br>– short term<br>– aggressivity of the criteria<br>– growth targets and ambitious sales objectives/targets<br>– the parents' attitude towards the role of the JV general manager on:<br>• source/scope of his authority<br>• status<br>• personality vs. position<br>• responsibility for decision-making<br>• responsibility for future events |

| Question | Developing countries | Developed countries |
|---|---|---|
| 14. How is the JV general manager's performance evaluated? | on the basis of several factors related to his ability:<br>– to meet parents' expectations<br>– to achieve JV's objectives<br>– to maintain a good working relation with managers from parents' organization<br>– to master cross-cultural communication issues/ problems with local expatriates and with partner's headquarters | on the basis of several factors related to his ability:<br>– to meet parents' expectations<br>– to achieve JV's objectives<br>– to maintain a good working relation with managers from parents' organizations<br>– to master cross-cultural communication issues/ problems in developed countries |
| 15. Why is it difficult for the JV general manager to meet parents' expectations? | – parent organizations have different sets of expectations from the JV<br>– these expectations are seldom fully communicated to the JV general manager<br>– these communications are seldom fully understood because of different cross-cultural perceptions<br>– these expectations change over time<br>– there is a certain reluctance to make these expectations clear because<br>– there is an element of fear that by making them clearly communicated and well perceived cross-culturally, bargaining power/position in dealing with the partner would weaken | – parent organizations have different sets of expectations from the JV<br>– these expectations are seldom fully communicated to the JV general manager<br>– these communications are seldom fully understood because of different cross-cultural perceptions to be reconciled<br>– these expectations change over time<br>– there is a certain reluctance to make these expectations clear because<br>– there is an element of fear that by making them clearly communicated and well perceived cross-culturally, bargaining power/position in dealing with the partner would weaken. |
| 16. What are the intervening negative factors which make a TC opt for a JV? | | – TC's inaccurate perception of government suasive pressure to form the JV<br>– just try it out, i.e. TC agree to form JV in a peripheral business to which it has no commitment |

(*Continued*)

| Question | Developing countries | Developed countries |
|---|---|---|
| | | – satisfy TC's executive personal needs, *vis-à-vis* corporate evaluation system by returning home with a signed contract<br>– TC's internal evaluation and reward system may overemphasize "beating the bushes" for new area of operation; thus encouraging the JV formation<br>– executives cannot travel extensively without something to show for to justify travel costs, market studies, time invested, personal investigative work<br>– TC's impatience for results over the short term |
| 17. What pitfalls are there? | – to enter a JV agreement when everything hinges on acquiring new technologies | – to enter a JV agreement for organizational and individual pressures rather than strategic and economic reasons |
| 18. When is sharing in a JV a bad deal? | – whenever it is euphemistically viewed as a sharing of risks without a full understanding that<br>– benefits will not be harvested without an harmonious decision-making process fully shared by both partners through the JV general manager | – whenever it is euphemistically viewed as a sharing of risks without a full understanding that<br>– strategies and economic benefits will not be harvested without<br>– appropriate implementation and adequate solutions for difficulties to come, while the initial rationale may change because of practical difficulties in implementing designed strategy |
| 19. How does one characterize the decision to join a partner in a JV agreement? | – necessary to fully implement the newly designed export-oriented policies | – possibly one of the most important decisions<br>– it is certainly one of the most difficult and time consuming. |

| Question | Developing countries | Developed countries |
|---|---|---|
| 20. How not to select a partner for a business venture? | – do not take the first partner that comes along, i.e. fortuitous meetings, cocktails, bars, hotels, etc.<br>– introduction confused with recommendation<br>– mistakenly trading poor partner's quality for quick action<br>– selected for political reasons | – do not take the first partner that comes along, i.e. fortuitous meetings, cocktails, bars, hotels, etc.<br>– introduction confused with recommendation<br>– mistakenly trading poor partner's quality for quick action<br>– selected for short-term political reasons<br>– impatience leading to a careless selection process |
| 21. How to select a partner for a business venture? | – establish clearly motivations and expectations of both parties<br>– be aware of possible problems created by the size differential of the two businesses<br>– visit potential partner in his milieu/country<br>– invite potential partner to visit your milieu in (for him) foreign country<br>– work on a small project to test compatibility<br>– TC will probably interact with prominent families in host country — because of their culture, family interests ahead of national business development; therefore, local partner has to help TC Reps to understand with whom in the family he will be working | what to look for:<br>– a local industrial entrepreneur who can<br>– bring knowledge of local economy, politics, culture<br>– supply the JV general manager<br>– help the TC in continuous learning process of the host country's culture<br>– help expatriate personnel to be integrated into the local community and not become insulated with the local expatriate community<br>– find a firm offering complementary services, i.e. distribution network<br>– make sure he knows who in the family within the host country is the possible silent leader |
| 22. On what principles to base a sound JV? | – fair exchange<br>– value for both parties<br>– mutual need and commitment<br>– regular communication<br>– regular co-operation | – fair exchange<br>– value for both parties<br>– mutual need and commitment<br>– regular communication<br>– regular co-operation |
| 23. When is commitment required? | – at each step in the JV process<br>– to overcome initial uncertainties in a new country and new partner | – at each step in the JV process<br>– to overcome initial uncertainties in new country and new partner |

(*Continued*)

| Question | Developing countries | Developed countries |
|---|---|---|
| 24. What is commitment? | – the single most critical factor in entering a new foreign market<br>– the most important attribute to staying in the newly entered market and in the ongoing management of a JV | – a challenge<br>– an important value in any TC<br>– the vehicle to be used to run on the road of problems/difficulties in the JV and reach agreed and acceptable solution<br>– to visit the JV from TC headquarters when serious problems arise<br>– to supply JV with special skills whenever needed |
| 25. How commitment is expressed? | – financial resources<br>– to customers<br>– to partner's support<br>– to product integrity<br>– to never ending process of learning about doing business on the international scene<br>– to the never ending process of building trust and sharing information with partner<br>– to co-operative relationship<br>– but not forgetting that as a JV it has a life of its own as long as *both* partners keep on making an active contribution thus expressing their renewed commitment<br>– including TC partner in discussions even if not required by agreement<br>– holding regular meetings<br>– share decision-making processes per the designed JV; however, realize that consensus decision is time consuming and may lead to conflict; therefore<br>– decisions are made by the JV general manager, sensitive to the other partner's needs and culture, willing to understand, learn and be persuaded as well as being persuasive. Decisions could be alternatively split between partners according to knowledge, etc. | – to employees round the world<br>– to partner support financial resources<br>– to the never ending process of learning about host country politics, culture, etc.<br>– to the never ending process of building trust and sharing information with partner<br>– to build a co-operative relationship<br>– by not keep making decisions for TC's headquarters as if JV were a wholly-owned subsidiary<br>– by never considering the possibility of quitting while facing difficult problems<br>– including local partner in discussions even if not required by JV agreement<br>– keeping partner informed at all times |

| Question | Developing countries | Developed countries |
|---|---|---|
| 26. How to design the JV's structure? | – partners determine the content of the agreement<br>– general agreement and expectations have been made clear by both partners<br>– commitment by both partners has been secured<br>– commitment by both partners' spokespersons/CEO then<br>– call in/hire the best local lawyer and accounting firm to help with the legal and financial structuring of the JV in accordance with the law of the host country | same |
| 27. Where not to start looking in difficult times? | – local partner blames<br>• TC partner<br>• international situation<br>• change in the local political climate<br>• change in the local economy caused by the international business climate | – TC blames<br>• local partner<br>• local government<br>• general state of the economy<br>• anyone else<br>• technological foot dragging, i.e. TC becomes upset with the course of co-operation agreement to share technology to market product locally and begins to drag feet in the next generation of technology |
| 28. Where to start looking when facing difficult times? | at oneself | at oneself |

# Recommended Reading and Intelligence Resources

European business people interested in educating themselves on Asian political and business affairs are advised to follow the work being carried out by international institutions such as: the Hanns Seidel Foundation, in Munich, Germany, the Asia Society, found in major cities of Asia, the Südasien Institute in Heidelberg, Germany, the Institute of Strategic Studies in Jakarta, Indonesia, the Institute of Southeast Asian Studies in Singapore, the Malaysian Institute of Strategic Studies in Kuala Lumpur, the ISESAO at Bocconi University in Milan, Italy, the Royal Institute of International Affairs, London, England, the Chambre de Commerce et d'Industrie de Paris ASEAN Bureau, Paris, France, Nordic Association of Asian Studies, Copenhagen, Denmark.

Another valuable source of information is international conferences organized by international publications such as *The Economist*, the *Wall Street Journal*, the London *Financial Times*, the *European Management Journal*, and the *International Herald Tribune*, as well as by the HEC Eurasia Institute, Paris, the Agnelli Foundation, Turin, Italy, the European Round Table of Industrialists, Brussels, the Nordic Institute of Asian Studies, the Euro-Asia Management Studies Association, the ISESAO, the INSEAD Euro-Asia Centre, Paris, the School of Oriental Studies in London, and the London Business School.

The following newspapers, journals, and books are also invaluable sources of information:

## NEWSPAPERS AND JOURNALS

The *Nikkei Weekly*; the Australian *National Business Week*; the Singapore *Straits Times*; the Singapore *Business Times*; the Malaysian *New Straits Times*; the *Times* (Indonesia); *Kompass*; *The Bulletin*; *The Bangkok Post*, *Business* (Thailand); *Asia Age*; *Asia Week*; *South*; The *Far Eastern Economic Review*; *Asia Inc.*; *Asia Money*; *Capital*; *Wirtschaftswoche*; *The Economist*; the London *Financial Times*; the *International Business Week*; the *International Herald Tribune*; The *Wall Street Journal* (US, European and Asian editions); *Eurobusiness*; *Business Age*; *Le Monde Diplomatique*; *Le Figaro*; *Blick durch die Wirtschaft*; *Power in Asia FT Newsletter*; *Asia Infrastructure Monthly*; *Foreign Affairs*.

## BOOKS


Abbegglen, James C., *Sea Change: Pacific Asia as the New World Industrial Centre*, New York Free Press, New York, 1994.

Agarwala, Damunap, "The role of investment incentives in East–West competition in ASEAN countries", *Indian Economic Journal*, volume 68, no. 269, pp. 223–238; 1987

Australian's Dept. of Foreign Affairs and Trade, The East Asia Analystical Unit; *Overseas Chinese Business Networks in Asia*; Melbourne, 1995.

Bloodwoth, Dennis, *The Profile of an Opportunity: The Risks and Rewards of Investing in China*, Times Academic Press, Singapore, 1995.

Bresnan, John, *From Dominos to Dynamos: The Transformation of South East Asia*, Council on Foreign Relations Press, New York, 1994.

Cheong Mei Sui and Adibah Amin, *Daim: The Man Behind the Enigma*, Pelanduk Publications, Petalying Jaya, Malaysia, 1995.

Conklin, Jeffrey Scott, *Forging an East Asian Foreign Policy*, Lanham, MD, University Press of America, 1995.

Dobbs-Higginson, M. S., *Asia Pacific its Role in the New World Order*, Mandarin, London, 1995.

EIU, "Singapore 2003: Aspiring to the First World", *The Economist*, London 1995.

Heritage Foundation, The, *Why Asia Grows and Africa Doesn't*, The Heritage Foundation, Washington D.C., 1990.

Hersh, Jacques, *The USA and the Rise of East Asia Since 1945*, Macmillan, London, 1993.

Hobday, Michael, *Innovation in East Asia the Challenge to Japan*, Edward Elgar, Aldershot, Hants, 1995.

James, David L. *The Executive Guide to Asia Pacific Communications*, Allen & Unwin, St. Leonards, Australia, 1995.

Jomo, K. S., *Japan and Malaysian Development in the Shadow of the Rising Sun*, Routledge, London, 1995.

Khoo Boo Teik, *Paradoxes of Mahathirism*, Oxford University Press, Shah Alam, Malaysia, 1995.

Lassere, Philippe and Schutte, Helmut, *Strategies for Asia Pacific*, MacMillan Business, New York, 1995.

Lat, *Lat 30 Years Later*, Petalying Jaya, Malaysia, 1995.

Leifer, Michael, *Dictionary of Modern Politics of South East Asia*, Routledge, London, 1995.

Lloyd George, Robert, *The East–West Pendulum*, Woodhead-Faulkner Ltd, Cambridge, UK, Simon & Shuster International Group, 1992.

Mahatir, Mohamad and Shintaro Ishihara, *The Voice of Asia: Two Leaders Discuss the Coming Century* Leifer, Michael, Kodansha International, Tokyo, 1995.

Naisbit, John, *Megatrends Asia*, Nicholas Brealey, New York, 1995.

OECD, *New Dimensions of Market Access in a Globalising World Economy*, OECD, Paris, 1994.

Randlesome, Colin, *Business Cultures in Europe*, Butterworth-Heinemann, Oxford, 1993.

Rower, Jim, *Asia Rising*, Butterworth-Heinemann, Singapore, 1995.

Sanjyot P. Dunung, *Doing Business in Asia*, Simon & Schuster, Singapore, 1995.

Seagrave, Sterling: *Lord of the Rim*, Bantam Press, New York, 1995.

Steiner, Henry and Haas, Ken, *Cross-Cultural Design Communicating in the Global Market-place*, Thames & Hudson, 1995.

Sutter, Robert, *East Asia and the Pacific Challenges for the US Policy*, Westview Press, Boulder, Co., 1995.

World Bank: *The East Asian Miracles*, Oxford University Press, New York, 1993.

UNCTAD Division on Transnational Corporations and Investment. Small and medium-sized transnational corporations: *Role, Impact and Policy Implications*, New York, Geneva, 1993.

UNCTAD Division on Transnational Corporations and Investment, *Multilateral Investment Instruments: A Compendium*, New York, Geneva, 1996.

# Index

Note: Page references in *italics* refer to Figures; those in **bold** refer to Tables

*Index compiled by Annette Musker*

**JOHN WILEY & SONS LTD**

WILEY

**Listen to the Emerging Markets of Southeast Asia/Letta**

To receive details of new Wiley publications in your area of interest please complete this card. We will send you a FREE Business & Management catalogue.

Name ______________________________

Position ______________________________

Organisation ______________________________

Address ______________________________

______________________________

Country ______________ Post/zip code ______________

Telephone: ______________ Fax: ______________ e-mail: ______________

Areas of interest: ______________________________

______________________________

Where did you buy this book:
- ❑ Bookshop ______________ *(Please specify)*
- ❑ Direct from Wiley
- ❑ Other ______________ *(Please specify)*

***By air mail***
***Par avion***

IBRS/CCRI NUMBER:
PHQ-D/1204/PO

NE PAS AFFRANCHIR

NO STAMP REQUIRED

REPONSE PAYEE
GRANDE-BRETAGNE

Jo Underwood
John Wiley & Sons Ltd
Baffins Lane
CHICHESTER
West Sussex,
GREAT BRITAIN
PO19 1YN